Pre-publication Revi

"David Markay is a listener to the heart: only a pastor with deep caring for his people – all of them – could bring us these reflections. Emerging out of seven years of costly identification with an interracial congregation of immigrant and indigenous Italian Christians, they provide a unique handbook for learners of hospitality and grace. Ordinary people struggling to find each other over their divides, become extraordinary witnesses to the mysterious bridging power of Christ's love. This book is a must-read for congregations serious about being truly inclusive and for those who want to come nearer to Jesus and his longing to heal our fractured world".

Peter Storey, South African Methodist pastor, bishop and seminary teacher

ርያ

"One of the great challenges the contemporary church faces is the challenge of being as multicultural as the Kingdom of God. Dave Markay helps us to expand the reach of God's gracious embrace in our congregations with his firsthand account of leading multicultural congregations. This is an encouraging and helpful book!"

Will Willimon, United Methodist bishop, retired, and Professor of the Practice of Christian Ministry, Duke Divinity School, Durham, North Carolina, USA

ርያ

"David Markay shares from his incredible spectrum of experiences and insights. Each story catches the reader by surprise in its beginning, with no predictability for where it will end. He makes one see more and think more deeply. A book that does this is a book worth reading".

Üllas Tankler, Estonian Methodist pastor, Executive Secretary for Europe and North Africa, United Methodist General Board of Global Ministries

ርያ

"This book is a moving testimony of life and faith, a piece of personal and communal history which is interwoven with a thousand stories -- small and large, sad and happy -- from an increasingly globalized world. It reflects the struggles and joys, hopes and tensions, expectations and frustrations, grandeur and misery of the many men and women who come from every part of the world that, within the small Methodist and Waldensian churches in Italy, have chosen "To Be the Church Together": not an easy slogan, not an abstract theory, but a steep and complex existential challenge to live side by side....

…This process is transforming different traditions, cultures, liturgical and theological sensitivities, offering a precious opportunity for all involved to reconsider their vocations, knowledge and vision, to learn new languages of faith, and to move toward a continuous renewal of individual and communal identities. Thanks to David Markay (and to Kristin, Hannah and Aidan) for having offered their many gifts and their way of seeing – intelligent and attentive, affectionate and critical – in the service of our churches!"

Alessandra Trotta, President, Opera per le Chiese Evangeliche Metodiste in Italia (The Methodist Church in Italy)

ଔ

"With its empathetic curiosity, "Pasta and Plantains" has much to offer to churches and organizations that are grappling with the joys and challenges of multicultural diversity. As the Methodist Church in Britain journeys toward true inclusion, it too can learn from David Markay's insightful book".

Lia Dong Shimada, Learning and Development Officer, The Methodist Church in Britain.

ଔ

PASTA AND PLANTAINS

PASTA AND PLANTAINS

Being the Church Together

~

when everything else
would keep us apart

First published in Great Britain in 2013 by

Bannister Publications Ltd
118 Saltergate
Chesterfield
Derbyshire S40 1NG

Typeset in Minion Pro and designed by Escritor Design
Chesterfield, Derbyshire

Printed and bound in the UK by SRP Ltd, Exeter

For Hannah and Aidan

Who, in our seven-year experience in Italy, had to cross many more barriers than did their Mom and Dad – not without difficulty, but with a grace and humour that helped those around them, especially their parents, to do it better. *Grazie, ragazzi.*

Acknowledgements

I am grateful to everyone who gave me feedback on these words and coaxed them into print: Jon Adams (whose suggestion for a title 'The Pasta-Driven Life' was overruled), Keith Bailey, Phillip Borkett, Eliana Briante, Bob and Carla Chiles, Moira Cram, George Ennin, Christine Erb-Kanzleiter, Nancy Feyen, Brian Fish, Pamela Grayson, David Jenkins, Aidan Markay (who suggested, 'The Plantain Strikes Back'), Hannah Markay ('Pasta and Prejudice'), Jeff Markay and Julie Yarborough, Roger and Lou Markay, Mary Anne Morefield, Michael and Åsa Nausner, Helen Neinast, Elymas Newell, Doug Renalds, Lia Shimada, Michael Steibli, Peter Storey, Üllas Tankler, Alessandra Trotta, Hans Växby and Will Willimon.

The United Methodist General Board of Global Ministries, through the backing of numerous congregations in the United States, supported our family during our fifteen years of service in Lithuania, New York and Italy.

Tom Blyth of Bannister Publications Ltd in Chesterfield, England, crossed several barriers, both cultural and grammatical, to bring this book to print. I am indebted to his attention to detail and delight in words.

Over many a shared *cappuccino*, my wife Kristin has discussed, read and corrected this manuscript with me. Someone has said that Jesus sent people out in twos, not only to support one another but also so that later, they could reflect together upon all their experiences. That God arranged it so that I could do all that with the person I love most is a gift of grace.

Introduction

If you think you've picked up a cookbook, put it down quickly and get to a different section of the bookstore. If you're on-line, click elsewhere.

Chances are that pasta and plantains would not find themselves together in too many recipes in Italy, Asia, Africa or elsewhere. The Italians, known for their particularity about food, might politely wag a finger as if to say "*Non si fa,*" ("It is not done"). Plantains *with* pasta?! A tropical vegetable-banana in a Mediterranean diet? Perhaps on separate plates or as a different course. But heaven forbid, not served together.

Just before we think the Italians a bit unyielding on matters of food, think of a Brit's reaction to an American staple, peanut butter and jam on the *same* sandwich! But the American responds with a sceptical grimace to baked beans *on top of* toast. Guidelines, informed by years of tradition, are clear. Some things go together. Others do not.

Put the people who hold these strong opinions together around the same table, and things get tricky. Most of us have our own set of 'it is not done' standards of normalcy. Jesus, however, invites us to a new kind of table fellowship. He has a way of reshuffling and rewriting our most tried and true recipes. This book is a reflection on how the Gospel of Jesus joins together what we may have always thought to be separate.

Our family lived in Milano from 2004 until 2011. My wife Kristin and I, supported by the United Methodist General Board of Global Ministries, served as ministers in two intercultural Italian Methodist congregations.

The following meditations reflect the lives of those communities – made up of people of different cultures, languages, temperaments, church traditions, and (at last count) eighteen different countries – trying to live together. The societal backdrop is Italy, a nation struggling with the issues of immigration and integration. The urban context is primarily Milano, Novara and other cities whose resources and patience are being stretched by the influx of foreigners. The ecumenical setting is a predominantly Roman Catholic country in which many churches are seeking to offer hospitality to the stranger. The missional motto that guides the Italian Methodist-Waldensian Church is a desire, not only to welcome the outsider, but to blend traditions and to be changed by the other – 'essere la chiesa insieme' ('to be the church together').

Beyond Jesus' high priestly prayer for his disciples to live as one, beyond a general consensus that unity is a pretty good idea, and beyond a catchy church slogan of togetherness, this collection of stories presents a group of people trying to do the daily work of living in Christian community. The best way to read this book may be to sample it a bit at a time. I would suggest the gentle reading style of *lectio divina*, attentive enough to enter into each meditation or chapter, but receptive enough to pause and digest… perhaps inspiring you to a recipe or two in your own context.

The stories and images are meant as a tribute to the congregations we served. Where necessary I have changed names and circumstances to protect privacy…. but hopefully not so much as to prevent individuals from recognizing themselves or from feeling my deep admiration for their Christian witness.

David Markay
Dronfield, England

Contents

*"Father, protect them in your name that you have given me,
so that they may be one, as we are one."*
Jesus

"Real community is painful."
Jean Vanier

*"Everybody wants to live together.
Why can't we be together?"*
Sade Adu

Hardly Together

"...the psalms teach us to pray as a fellowship. The Body of Christ is praying, and as an individual one acknowledges that his prayer is only a minute fragment of the whole prayer of the Church... Many of the psalms were very probably prayed antiphonally in the Old Testament community. The so-called 'parallelism of the members', that remarkable repetition of the same sense in different words in the second line of the verse, is not merely a literary form; it also has import for the Church and theology ... Often in the psalms there are two voices, bringing the same concern to God."

Dietrich Bonhoeffer, *Life Together* (1)

Often in worship the congregation reads a psalm responsively and bilingually, alternating languages on each verse ...   ➤➤

Give ear to our words, O Lord.	✦	*Give heed to our sighing.*
Some of us are reading in Italian.	✦	Some in Twi, Tagalog, English.
Our Bible.	✦	*Our* Bible.
Odd verses.	✦	Even verses.
A bit jumbled.	✦	Not always in unison.
Some of us haven't found the page yet.	✦	Others are reading from different versions.
Start.	✦	Stop.
Stop.	✦	Start.
Brief hesitation.	✦	Awkward waiting.
Words overlap.	✦	Seams do not meet.
Scusa.	✦	Sorry.
Please keep up.	✦	Please slow down.
Do they still have more to read?	✦	Is that the end of the verse?
Mistakes?	✦	Spaces of grace?
Are we interlocking?	✦	Or are we parallel?
Hard to hear my part among all of *you.*	✦	Hard to hear my part among all of *you.*
Do we sound loud enough?	✦	Do we sound a bit weak?
You're odd.	✦	*I'm* odd?
Am I listening to your voice?	✦	Am I only hearing my own?
Do you listen when I read the verses?	✦	Or are you only preparing for your verse?
Do I pay attention only to my language?	✦	Do I seek to understand yours?
Do our words sound united?	✦	Or do they sound separate?
Are we members?	✦	Or are we a community?
Two voices praying at once?	✦	Or just two voices?
Are we one?	✦	Or merely together?
Give ear to our words, O Lord.	✦	*Give heed to our sighing.*

*"When an alien resides with you in your land,
you shall not oppress the alien.*

*The alien who resides with you shall be to you
as the citizen among you;*

*you shall love the alien as yourself;
for you were aliens in the land of Egypt:*

I am the Lord your God."

Leviticus 19:33-34

"I had gone out jogging. The carabinieri stopped me. I do not know what for. Well, actually, I do know. It is hard for me to hide my Asian face. They asked me for my documents. I did not have my wallet, but fortunately I had stuck my passport in my pocket. I have learned to do that now, almost by instinct."

"They told me I could live with them, prepare meals for their family. But they said that I should not eat before them, nor should I make any extra food for myself. If there is extra, they will tell me if I can have it. This one day, there was one last fillet on the serving plate. Just a little one. No one had eaten it. The signora said, "Wrap that up and put it in the freezer. One of us will have it next time.""

"An African teenager living in Parma returned to his family late one night, his face swollen and bruised, one eye bloodshot and nearly closed. He had been in police custody, allegedly mistaken for a drug dealer. When the police released him, they handed him a white envelope containing his wallet, which they had confiscated.

On the envelope was written 'Emmanuel – Negro'."

A 36-year-old Chinese immigrant living in Tor Bella Monaca near Rome was recently beaten by a group of Italian youths who had stopped him in the street. The gang, it turns out, had beaten an African immigrant earlier in the week. The Chinese man was photographed in his hospital bed, his nose broken and chin cut. The blood-stained T-shirt he had been wearing at the time of the attack is typical of those on sale at Chinese markets, with nonsense English words made to look like a fancy brand name. The words on this particular T-shirt read: 'Each Person Dances', and just below that: 'WATCHING YOU'.

Watching you. Could be a silk-screened message to a country's aching moral conscience.

*"By the rivers of Babylon – there we sat down
and there we wept when we remembered Zion."*

Psalm 137:1

Everyone around the table looked tired. Some had arrived at church this morning, having only left work an hour earlier. Others had finished their labours near midnight the night before. The Bible study, about exile, reflected our collective lack of energy. It was getting bogged down in a list of kings and invasions; talk of Babylon in the sixth century BC, songs of Zion, Nebuchadnezzar, Edomites, and longing for the holy city. It did not seem to be speaking to anyone this morning.

Exile, someone read aloud from the guidebook, was where the Judahites found themselves; far from Jerusalem, from their holy place and from their home. They were mocked by their captors and urged to sing songs of 'mirth'. Babylon was a place of grief and humiliation. Exile, he continued reading, can be *a place, a condition, a setting in which we don't want to be…*

Alicia let out a little sigh. Her lip began to quiver, and she reached for a tissue. Someone put a hand on her shoulder.

"I'm sorry," she sniffled. "I didn't mean to interrupt the lesson."

"What is it?" asked one of her friends.

"Oh, you know my work situation. I had such a difficult week. I'm sorry if this is not what we are talking about. I am just so… so discouraged. My *signora*, she yells at me so much. She asked me to prepare a meal, and I couldn't remember how I had done it the last time. She was so angry. She called me such terrible things."

She blew her nose. "I am tired of waking up in the morning and wondering what kind of mood my employer will be in. Will she be kind today? Will she be harsh today? I pray to God, please give me patience. Please, God, make the heart of my *signora* more gentle."

"Sometimes, I just think of putting all of my things in a bag and going home. If I could, I would just walk away from her. But then I think of all the people I am sending money to. At home, they would not understand. They are waiting on the money I send to them. My cousins, my mother, my sisters and brothers, my aunt; they need what I make."

"It feels…" she said, "it feels like I am in prison."

"I'll meet you on the ridge between these worlds apart."

Bruce Springsteen (2)

Captain America climbs the mound of dirt. His father waits at the bottom with his little brother, who is dressed as a circus clown. As the sun sets on this February Sunday, his cape casts a tiny shadow on the soccer field, where early spring mud is kicked up to shouts in Arabic.

His mother calls him back to the bench. She reaches in a plastic sack filled with confetti, and hands him a fistful.

The defender blocks the ball with his chest. It hits the *Al Ittihad Dubai* jersey logo and drops to his feet. Clearly the leader, he motions to his teammates forward, then lofts a kick over the half-way line.

The captain descends the hill and tosses a handful of Carnevale fun into the air. Pink and green specks flutter down onto the soccer pitch. The father motions to let the ones over the line lie where they fall.

A pass scoots up-field, sending a puff of white chalk from the out-of-bounds line. A young striker, with dark hair and olive skin, flashes past the caped crusader, taps the ball with his foot, keeping it in bounds.

The superhero prepares for a fast descent off his perch. His father motions for him to stay clear of the game and to run back to his mother on the park bench.

No contact, no foul. No interference. No clash of cultures; not even a bump. One park, two worlds. But for a stray kick or a disobedient child, these captains and their teams will never meet.

*"With joy and thanksgiving we welcome you as
a member of the family of Christ."*

Baptismal Covenant I,
United Methodist Book of Worship (3)

The tiny infant squirmed as his mother held her near the baptismal font. A little tuft of dark hair poked out from beneath her bonnet. Her dark tan face and brown eyes peeked over her mother's arm, staring at the family gathered around. She was surrounded by a small army of godfathers and godmothers, all – in the Filipino tradition – holding lit candles.

Just beyond the circle around her, one of the elderly Italian women of the congregation looked on. I could only imagine that she was recalling the baptisms of her children and grandchildren at this same font. Recently, she has seen more baptisms of children whose names she would have trouble pronouncing; fewer Italian babies. Part of the reason is the demographic tide of immigrants entering Italy. The other is the declining Italian birth rate.

According to recent statistics, the average modern Italian family has one child. Roughly one-quarter of Italian women today have no children. The birth rate in many regions of the country is about half the death rate. Successive governments have tried to encourage families to have more children, recently introducing a 'baby bonus' of nearly $2,000 as an incentive. However, many couples realize that such a sum would not cover the rising costs of child care, medical coverage, food and schooling. So they keep their families small. The city schools that were once full are now half-empty, or are being filled with children of immigrants.

"In Italy they don't have children," noted one immigrant woman, "they have dogs and cats." (4)

Many Italians are alarmed that if the trend continues, not only will the country's population appear a lot different, not only will there be gaps in the area of labour and services, but that a truly *Italian* culture will continue to erode. Similar fears creep into parishes and congregations like ours.

As I looked at the Italian *nonna* on the front row, I wondered what she was thinking. The liturgy tells her to feel 'joy and thanksgiving'. What else is she feeling?

"…she got a papyrus basket for him,
and plastered it with bitumen and pitch;
she put the child in it among the reeds on the bank of the river.
His sister stood at a distance to see what would happen to him."

Exodus 2:3-4

Three weeks after giving birth, she had done the necessary paper work to acquire a passport for her baby. Then she bought a plane ticket and prepared for the twenty-hour journey back to her home village. She would leave her child there with family and then return to Italy to resume work. The child would be cared for by relatives. Someday, bureaucracies in both countries willing, she may be reunited with her child. But for the foreseeable future they will be 7,000 miles apart.

The Sunday before her departure, we prayed a prayer of dedication for the child. The baptism will occur back the mother's home in a few weeks. After worship, several immigrant members were talking about her decision:

"I tried to talk her out of it," said one woman. "She will regret what she is doing."

"How can we blame her?" said another. "Several of us left our children. We know there is no way we could make the money we need to raise them if we were back there. You know what unemployment is like at home."

"I left my children in the hands of relatives when I left 15 years ago," one man commented. "Unfortunately, many children like mine are left without much supervision. We parents abroad send money home for them, so often they have many things, but not a mother or a father there to guide them. My children are now teenagers. They have made some unwise choices. If I were to do it again, I would first ask myself: which is better, making enough money to support them through school and put food on their table, or being poor yet being there with them? I think I would choose to be with them."

Thousands of years earlier, another foreign woman placed a baby in a basket and pushed it gently into the current. Because we already know the end of that story, it seems a foregone conclusion that the basket will be retrieved, the baby lifted out and raised with love. But what if the basket had floated past its intended recipient? What if it had become lost in the reeds? On whose shore would it have landed? And the child inside? How would he have grown up?

As we dedicated the child, we could only pray, wonder, and then *stand at a distance to see what would happen to him.*

"By the roadside you sat… sat like a nomad in the desert."

Jeremiah 3:2 (NIV)

Across the street from the middle school, it's almost time for the morning bell to ring.

A man stands with his 12-year-old. She is wearing a heavy backpack and clutches the straps next to her chest. With one hand, she reaches up to her cheek and wipes away some tears. He digs in his pocket and finds a handkerchief to give her. He speaks to her softly in a language unknown to the other parents and children who scurry past. She bows her head, leans into his chest, and burrows. He cups her head in his hands, strokes her hair and talks to her gently. She shakes her head firmly.

The bell sounds across the street. *"Ciao! Buona scuola! Un baccione!"* ("Bye Bye! Have a good day at school! I'm sending you a big kiss!") shout the other parents. The girl looks across the street, but doesn't budge. Her father gently pulls her head to his chest again. He looks skyward, then at his watch.

Some day she may be speaking Italian with the other children. But before that day comes, she will walk through those doors many times by herself. She will routinely be taken out of class for language lessons. She will come to know other foreign children, but they will only be able to communicate with one another when they all learn Italian. She may not smile as much as she used to. Most likely she will be the brunt of teasing and, sadly, will learn words that bruise. She will know the feeling of sitting in class as if in a fog, unfamiliar words swirling around her head. She will stare blankly at the teacher when asked a question. She will come to expect laughter when she tries to answer and she may stop trying to answer because of it. Her confidence in herself may slide. Her personality, her expressiveness, her sense of humour may be hidden behind a mask. When the day ends, she may watch the other girls pair up, and wonder if she will ever have friends here. Hopefully, one of them will turn and smile and speak to her.

She may make it here. She may become more Italian than her parents. Then again, she may not. She may beg her parents to let her return to China to live with her grandparents.

Hers is the young face of globalisation.

"…you have set my feet in a broad place…"

Psalm 31:8

She asked me where the photo hanging on the office wall had been taken. "Oh, I took that in Bologna… back when I was twenty," I answered.

"Oh," she responded with a slight smile, "When I was about twenty, I also spent time in Bologna."

She told me how she had obtained a tourist visa in the Philippines for a trip to Budapest. After only two days, she and some friends left their tourist hotel. They had never intended to be tourists. They had friends already in Bologna, and that northern Italian city became their destination.

Other than submitting my passport number to the overseas studies office, I did nothing to make my travel or visa arrangements. My parents drove me to Kennedy Airport, where the 25 other college students gathered for our non-stop flight to Italy. A meal and a movie later, we arrived at Malpensa Airport where the director of our study programme was there to meet us. We boarded a chartered bus and, a snack and a bathroom break later, arrived in Bologna. We complained about having to lug our suitcases along two blocks of cobblestones. More university staff greeted us outside the school and shuttled us in taxis to our designated apartments. My bed was already made. There was even some bread and fruit on the kitchen table.

She and her two friends had no money; nothing with which to buy a train or bus ticket. So they set out on foot through the city streets of Budapest. Through the outlying suburbs, across the mountains of eastern Hungary, into Austria, and on through the Alps.

I also visited Budapest that year of college. Two friends and I purchased couchette tickets for the weekend. We chipped in for a hotel room, sampled goulash and Hungarian beer, shopped in markets and visited museums.

They walked along the highway and along back roads. They slept where they could, mostly out doors. It was summer, so sleeping rough wasn't impossible, but when it rained, especially in the mountains, they froze.

I have a vague recollection that on our way back from Hungary, our train may have passed through Yugoslavia. But then again, it was night. I don't remember getting out of our bunk beds.

She wore a pair of light sandals when she had left home. The leather straps strained and eventually broke. The mud caked up so thickly on the soles of her shoes that, somewhere across the Italian border, they broke completely. She made the remainder of the journey on foot. "Pastor, when I walked into Bologna, I was in my bare feet!"

I had brought with me to Bologna a pair of white Nikes, a pair of hiking boots, some dressy leather shoes, and probably a pair of bathroom sandals. When my grandparents sent me a gift check that Christmas, I bought a pair of trendy white Velcro-strap tennis shoes.

Some twenty-plus years later, both our routes have led to Milano. We sit in the same church; she with her husband and child, me with my wife and children. She cleans a woman's house. I pastor a congregation. And when I hold the chalice before her, I can't help but look down at her shoes, and then my own.

"He asked me, "Son of Man, can these bones live?"
I said, "O Sovereign Lord, you alone know."

Ezekiel 37:3 (NIV)

American Christians often ask about the state of Christianity in Europe. With the decline of church attendance across western Europe, the growing trends of secularization in European society, reluctance to include any reference to Europe's Christian history in the constitution of the European Union, and the ascending influence of Islam on the continent, observers of Christianity have clear concerns.

In an article on early-twenty first century Christianity in Europe and America, Orthodox theologian David Hart suggests that many in Europe suffer from a kind of boredom. It is not a boredom of every-day life. Rather, it is a boredom on a higher plane – boredom with the mysteries of life itself.

> *A culture, a civilization, is only as great as the religious ideas that animate it; the magnitude of people's cultural achievement is determined by the height of its spiritual aspirations. One need only turn one's gaze to the frozen mires and fetid marshes of modern Europe, where once the greatest of human civilizations resided, to grasp how devastating and omnivorous a power metaphysical boredom is.*

The boredom, sadly, is evident here in Italy. Some people seem to carry the Christian message as a weight of history. Others appear to have lost any expectation that the Gospel has a relevant message to offer modern society. Many, caught up in the rush of work and play, of social commitments and search for work, of political discussion and philosophical debate, seem to have all questions answered. There is little mystery. David Hart continues:

> *The eye of faith presumes to see something miraculous within the ordinariness of the movement, mysterious hints of an intelligible order calling out for translation into artifacts, but boredom's disenchantment renders the imagination inert and desire tepid. (5)*

So, all the more exciting to see 'mysterious hints' of 'something miraculous' happening out of the eye of the camera: some 50,000 Christian young people descend upon Milano for the Taize gathering of prayer; a middle-aged father of three decides to go through a catechism class in order to enter the church; a parent decides on a church for his family because he is stirred by the preaching he hears from an Italian pastor; a young man decides to be baptized, much to the surprise of his family; a young woman trains for ministry with persons in prison; another breaks into tears when trying to describe his re-entry into the faith…

Metaphysical boredom is a challenge to the church. Do we add to the boredom or rise above it? Do we seal the debates or encourage them? Do we snuff the joy of discovery or enhance it? Do we lay down an additional layer of suffocating dullness or, by our message and preaching and service and searching, orient people to the 'miraculous within the ordinariness'?

"Strengthen the feeble hands,
steady the knees that give way…"

Isaiah 35:3 (NIV)

She was coming around the street corner as I approached it from the other direction. "Oh, hello pastor!" Her head was wrapped with a scarf, her face all but hidden in grey wool, making her look older than her age. She was a bit hunched over but carried no heavy bags, only a small purse. On an early-December afternoon, it was already dark. The only way I could make out her face was by the light of a red blinking neon Christmas star hanging from a sign from the corner *Tabacchi*.

"I'm on my way to a new job. I've only had it for eight days now."

"How is it going so far?" I asked.

"Well, I'm just thankful that I have the job. I'm caring for a little boy. He's 18 months old, so he's beginning to walk. That's good. I keep encouraging him to walk, because after the operations on my back, I just can't lift him.

"I had cared for that *vecchia signora* (elderly woman) for four years. And because she didn't have very good balance, she would fall quite often. You know when someone falls, you try to catch them. Oh, and it hurt me so." She put her palm on the small of her back. "I had to go the hospital. The doctor told me that from all my carrying groceries and walking with my signora, my disks were rubbing on each other too strong.

"While I was in the hospital, I said to my husband, 'I have been thinking. I would like to take classes to be an *infermiera*. Remember before we came to Italy, I had started my training?' But that was 17 years ago. I should start it again," I said. That has always been my dream, to be a nurse.

"I mentioned it to the doctor there at the hospital. He told me it's too late to do that. Too much lifting of patients, and with my back, I just couldn't do it. So, I have no choice. We have to pay for our daughter's schooling here. We haven't sent money to our families back home in some time, because I was in the hospital. So, now I take this job. They are a good family. They are good to me. I just don't want the little one to fall, because I can't lift him."

The pulses of pink light from the Christmas star overhead highlighted the dark rings under her eyes. Each interval of darkness, in turn, gave a glimpse of how she must have appeared in her younger days.

"Well, pastor, I must go. Greetings to your family! Bye, pastor." And she turned gingerly, careful of her sore back. "By the way, what Bible lesson will we hear on Sunday for Advent?"

"It's… uh… Isaiah 35," I answered.

"Oh, I'll look it up when I get home later tonight."

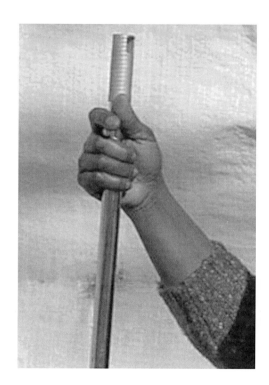

"one life is navy blue

one life is sunshine yellow

I am green."

Ruth Goring Stewart (6)

"Disorientation and uncertainty. Those," said the sociologist, "are two of the characteristics of immigrant youth." She noted that twenty-one in one hundred students in Milano are not Italians. "Some of these foreign youths were born somewhere else and are trying to adapt here," she said. "Others were born here, and feel fully Italian during the day... that is, until they go home. There, the parents still operate as guests in a foreign country. In one setting, people look at them as if they're strange. In the other, their parents may think they're becoming too Italian. For an adolescent, that's a lot to manage."

The presenter, an Italian, had conducted interviews with immigrant children throughout the country. The results of her research underscored the difficulty and complexity of being an adolescent and being a foreigner while living in Italy. "It's hard anywhere to be an adolescent," she said. "The period between ages fourteen and eighteen are when you are being formed as a person. So being an adolescent and being a foreigner can make for a difficult time."

"How would you characterize the life of an immigrant adolescent?" With a pointer, she tapped down a list of items on the screen behind her. "Few places in which they feel free to express themselves fully. Rare settings in which they are treated as equals. They often live with conflicts in the family, who struggle to manage life far from home. Sadly, with their parents working so hard, their lives often lack adult role models. They worry about the future."

"So, what do they need more than anything? Yes, *capitale sociale*." I asked my neighbour in a whisper what the term meant. He paused. "Allora ("Well, let's see")... it's like a wealth that you have around you; a big richness," he explained. "But it is not money, not material things. Is something like – how you say? Like a connection between people that... that... helps."

We turned back to the screen. "This *capitale sociale* needs to be enlarged and strengthened. Often the immigrant adolescent needs at least one place where they feel respected, welcomed, enjoyed for who they are. As they are growing in age, they need to grow in their values. Because their families are just not equipped to handle all the difficulties these young people face, they need to have adults in their lives other than their parents. These young people need a larger circle."

My neighbour nudged me. "Sounds like they need the church, huh?"

*"I have become a stranger to my kindred,
an alien to my mother's children"*

Psalm 69:8

Pastor, I want to share some news with you. Do you remember how I have waited to hear about my request for citizenship? I finally heard from the ministry of the interior.

Oh. What did they say?

They sent me the word this week. There are no more barriers for me to become a citizen. I just have to go down to the *Questura* and pick up the papers.

Well, I know you have been waiting for a long time. I'm glad your wait is over.

Ah yes, it is nice. It is what I have wanted for a long time. The process, it was not too difficult for me. Well, it is difficult for me. I mean to say, the Italian government did not make too big a problem for me. But the government in my country says that if I want to be an Italian citizen, I can no longer be a citizen there anymore. They do not grant double citizenship. I must choose. This is what I have wanted to do, but now I am finding that… that… how would I say it? I am a bit in the middle of the way.

Middle of the way?

Yes, that is where my parents still live. It is where I grew up. They said that it is up to me, this decision. They understand. I have lived away from them for many years. But I am a parent now, and my children will grow up here. I am no longer there. I am here. When I receive my new passport, I am going to have to give back my old passport. I still speak the language. I will always do, I think. It is not like I will forget my home, but I will no longer be a citizen there. I sometimes wonder if my children will ever want to visit. My parents think they will not want to. You see what I mean, being in the middle of the way?

Yes, this is quite a step for you. I wonder, maybe we could mark it in the church somehow… like saying a prayer for you in your new citizenship. What do you think?

Um. No, I don't really think we need to do that.

*"…strive to unite your voices together,
so as to make one melodious sound."*

John Wesley (7)

How am I
supposed to know
how they feel?
you say.
I'm *stonato*, deaf-to-tone,
you say;
I don't notice
things like that.

How did it happen?
Was it once there,
then lost?
Did some loud trauma
to your ears
muffle, deaden
the low frequencies,
or the high ones?
Is the damage irreversible?

Or have you selected
this deafness?
Is it laziness? Complacency?
But, then again,
tone is not a simple lesson.
Reading the notes
is a skill;
hearing them,
more a sense.

You march
while they sway.
You major
while they minor.
Their crescendo
is not on your sheet music.
Listen to it
over and over.
Maybe you'll hear it.

Summer's Eve on Via Fiori Oscuri

On one side	✦	On the other side
of the cobblestone	✦	of the cobblestone
trendy cafes,	✦	makeshift bazaar,
outdoor tables,	✦	box tops,
waiters	✦	salesmen
in black aprons.	✦	wearing T-shirts.
Customers,	✦	Vendors,
speak Italian,	✦	speak Senegalese,
English,	✦	Chinese,
Dutch.	✦	Arabic.
They appear oblivious	✦	They look intently
to the persons	✦	at the persons
on the other side,	✦	on the other side.
as though there is	✦	as possible sources
no connection.	✦	of income.
They chat,	✦	They chat,
they sip wine	✦	they share water
from glasses,	✦	from a bottle,
then sample the hors d'oevres	✦	then eat a sandwich
From a porcelain plate.	✦	from an aluminum wrap.

Tables,	✦	Tables,
covered with silk,	✦	covered with plastic,
lit candles,	✦	fake Gucci bags,
dessert spoon,	✦	imitation sunglasses,
elegant vase,	✦	fistful of flowers
that may hold	✦	that could be sold
a rose	✦	to a couple
from the Pakistanis	✦	of German tourists
across the street.	✦	across the street.
Wait for the bill;	✦	Wait for the diners to pay their bill;
then a stroll,	✦	then a hope
enjoying the evening that	✦	that this evening
might bring	✦	might bring
no rain,	✦	no police,
maybe a gelato.	✦	maybe a sale.

Together, in our Fears

"My child, do not forget my teaching..."

Proverbs 3:1

This space of concrete on the corner of Via Zuretti and Via Zuccoli has become a shrine. It was here, some months ago, that a murder had occurred, involving some Italians and some foreigners. The flowers that were placed here after the funeral are long gone. What has replaced them are flags of every political party and trade union. 'I'd rather be a *sporco negro* (*sporco* means dirty) than a blanking racist" said one. "*Negri* go back to Africa" said another.

Scribbled on a piece of loose-leaf paper and tucked between some candles was this message:

> *"Se i genitori di quei ragazzi avrebbero insegnato il rispetto per gli altri,tutto questo non fosse successo."* (*"If the parents of these guys had taught them to respect others, none of this would have happened."*)

I was struck by the words and took a small notebook out of my pack to jot them down. They seemed useful for a Sunday school lesson, as a sermon illustration, or a warning to parents against passing on racist attitudes to their children.

A man walking his dog stopped and looked. He nodded to me. "Did you know the guys?" he asked. "No," I answered, "I just wanted to see this place."

We stared at the wall some more. Then he motioned to my notebook and pen. "You a journalist or something?"

"No, but I wanted to remember one of these quotes."

"Oh, that one there about the parents needing to teach their children respect. It was placed there by somebody from a hate group. See their symbol at the bottom of the page?"

I hadn't noticed it. Now I was confused. *Hate group*? *Whose* parents? *Whose* children? Oh. Seems like this little patch of sidewalk had become something of battle site for the moral high ground... which all seems to make our work as parents that much more crucial.

"...I am convinced that men hate each other
because they fear each other.
They fear each because they don't know each other,
and they don't know each other because they don't communicate
with each other,
and they don't communicate with each other because
they are separated from each other."

Martin Luther King, Jr. (1)

One response to the influx of foreigners in Italy was the formation of a right-wing, nationalistic political party. Created in the early 1990s, the Lombard League, later called the Northern League (*Lega Nord*), advocated political autonomy and even independence for northern Italy. It has also taken on an increasingly strident anti-immigration message. Some of its recent campaigns have called for tighter laws on citizenship and have included picketing outside an Arab school in the city. One of its leaders provoked a firestorm by wearing an anti-Muslim T-shirt on television. Each year the *Lega* garners a sizeable portion of the vote, mostly in the north, where the impact of mass immigration is more pervasive. Its party headquarters rests only a mile or so from the *Chiesa Metodista* – a congregation filled with the kind of immigrants the *Lega* wants out.

The *Lega* has tapped into a growing strain of fear and anger in Italian society. In one northern Italian city, municipal leaders even erected a wall. While its stated purpose was to isolate drug traffic, protestors note that it divides the foreigners from the Italians. It has been dubbed *The wall of separation*. If separation is touted to bring less crime, less complication and more stability, it can be sold as an appealing option to people who are afraid of the demographic shifts going on around them.

One Milanese woman described to us the changes she has seen in her city. "It has happened so quickly," she said. "First, there were very few foreigners. Now there are so many. The change came so fast. Now I don't even recognize some of the places I once knew. Arab shops, Asian groceries, Moroccan coffee bars. I used to know all the proprietors of those places. Now I know none of them. I used to know all my neighbours. Now, with a lot of them, I can't even carry on a conversation."

Raising her hands in exasperation, she said, "We end up being caught somewhere between *paura* (fear) and the *voglia di* (the desire to)…" She continued to search for the right word, *"la voglia di… la voglia di capire* (the desire to understand)."

Not long after, I tested out her assessment on an Italian man in our congregation. He nodded. "Yes, we're all somewhere along that line, I guess. For example, six years ago when I looked at all the Filipinos in our church, all I saw was just a bunch of people with black hair. They were all running around talking in their language. To me they were just a big mob. None were speaking my language, and they were in my church! But one day after church I got to talking with Lena. She didn't speak Italian so well, but we were able to communicate. I found out that she has a sister in the congregation, and several cousins. She told me a few of their names, and how they're related. Over time, I'm getting to know them – not all of them, mind you, but enough that I'm able to ask individuals 'How's your son?' or 'Did you go to the doctor?' I know them better now as people."

Somewhere between fear and the desire to understand. Our natural tendencies pull us in one direction. Our Christian faith, hopefully, pulls us toward the other.

"…though the earth should change,
though the mountains shake in the heart of the sea…

Psalm 46:2-3

The neighbourhood council in San Siro is up in arms. City planners are contemplating a move for one of its landmarks. It seems that someone decided that the giant bronze horse that has stood outside the San Siro race track would look better near the city's Castello Sforzesco. *Il Cavallo di Leonardo* (Leonardo's Horse) has been keeping his mid-trot stance at his current home since 1999. He was a gift from American artists who had sculpted every muscle and hoof according to the ancient drawings of Leonardo da Vinci himself. It appears now, however, that its horse shoes are made for walking… So, some people in San Siro are yelling the Italian equivalent of "Hell no, don't let him go!"

As an outsider, I have to wonder what the fuss is all about. *Il Cavallo*, after all, is not an ancient fixture in that part of town. It would be understandable if people had photos of their grandparents and great-grandparents leaning on his hoof. But, it was only eight years ago that he ended up at the city's famous racetrack. So, when an interview with the spokesperson of the *Committee-to-keep-Leonardo's-Horse-right-where-he-already-is* appeared in the paper, I tried my best to understand her motives.

"The statue is doing well where it is," she began, "right here in this corner of the city. It gives dignity to this area." She continued: "What we fear is that this would be the first step for a total change to our neighbourhood. What will they want to do next? We're hearing about all kinds of speculation on other possible changes to our *zona*. When would it stop?"

Ah, there it is: *where would this one change lead?*

Italians, someone has said, are 'allergic to reform'. But then again, that committee member could be a spokesperson for all of us. A child whose family has recently moved becomes more attached to his parents and his stuffed animals. The pillar of the church shouts at the new member who is full of new ideas: "We make this change now. Then what will you want next? I won't be able to recognize my church any more!"

A change here portends a change there, and then where will it lead? What will become of my neighbourhood, my family, my church? What will become of me? The proverbial lid on Pandora's box is our guard – not just against a little untidiness, but against absolute chaos.

The earth changes. The mountains shake, and we can either hold fast to the things we think will give us stability, or Something more lasting.

"You shall not oppress a resident alien;
you know the heart of an alien,
for you were aliens in the land of Egypt."

Exodus 23:9

Recently, an incident of domestic violence involving a Pakistani family living in a northern Italian city, prompted a media furor. Pundits shouted that immigration was suffocating Italian culture. A prominent politician visited the city and proclaimed that Italy should now and always be "Italian and Catholic" – nostalgic words filled with potent political meaning.

The same week at a Waldensian Methodist gathering, the newly appointed Minister of Social Affairs was scheduled to speak. He had been invited several weeks earlier, not only as a politician, but as child of the church. He had grown up in the Waldensian Church in the Piemonte valleys and had publicly talked of his formation in a Protestant youth group. Part homecoming, part stump speech, he addressed the assembly on the issue of immigration.

"There was a time," he said, "when we Italians were a nation of emigrants; hardly any of us do not have a relative who moved to northern Europe, North or South America, or Australia. Even though that time of massive emigration has passed, we still tend to think of ourselves as a poor nation. It is time no longer to think of ourselves as the poor nation that sends immigrants, but as a wealthy country that can receive them. Are we poor and need help, or are we rich and can offer help? How we answer that question will effect the way we respond to the issue of immigration."

The Minister has clearly answered the question for himself, recently proposing an overhaul of Italy's immigration laws, essentially making citizenship a more attainable possibility. This change, he suggests, would help immigrants enter into Italian society legally and with a greater sense of responsibility and respect.

Referring to the case of the Pakistani family, he reminded us of the strains that immigration puts on a family. Not only do they experience economic pressures, but they struggle to maintain their ethnic identity in a society that is indifferent to their customs and traditions. "Who of us," he asked, "does not remember hearing about family strife among our emigrant relatives?"

"What did you think of the speech?" I asked one of the other attendees.

"Oh, he was great," he said. "Actually, I've known him since our youth. Did you know that his grandmother emigrated to the United States back in the 1920s? For several years she earned a living as a *badante* (a person who gives care to an elderly person). And interestingly, when his grandfather was an old man, it was a *badante* from Romania who cared for him."

*"When the messenger comes, see that you shut the door
and hold it closed against him.*

Is not the sound of his master's feet behind him?"

II Kings 2:32

His middle-eastern features and my *LL Bean* sweater made us both obvious foreigners in the assembly. Standing next to the crowded refreshment table, I introduced myself.

"*Mi chiamo* David."

"*Piacere*" (it's a pleasure) he responded, "I am Mansur. Where are you from?"

"The United States," I replied. "And you?"

"Iran," he said deliberately, "not Iraq… I-ran". We both smiled slightly and nodded.

After a pause, he asked, "And what are you doing in Milano?"

Relieved to avoid a discussion of geopolitics, I replied, "I am a Methodist pastor. I am here with my wife and fam…"

"Wait!" he interrupted. "Did you say you are a Methodist?"

"Yes."

"Isn't George Bush a Methodist?"

"Well, George Bush does belong to a Methodist congregation…"

He turned abruptly to two people near him, motioning them to come near. "This is David. He's a Methodist from the United States. like George Bush!"

"You know George Bush?" one friend said.

"No, not personally…."

"Yes," Mansur quipped (it was hard to tell if he was joking) "They're friends!"

"No, we're definitely not frien…"

"So you've been to the White House?" the friend continued, making giant leaps for mankind over the language gap between us.

"No, I hav…"

"And Mrs Bush, what is she like?"

"I'm not really su…"

"Well, the next time you go, please ask George Bush not to bomb Iran."

"Excuse me?"

"You tell him. At your next Methodist meeting, ask him that. Another sandwich?"

"God does not judge by external appearance"

Galatians 2:6 (NIV)

"Avoid Bus 91, if you can!" This was the advice from an Italian woman upon our arrival in Milano. When we asked her why, she explained that the bus which circles the city's ring road is "The foreigner bus." It also happens to run a convenient course, so we are often on it.

One afternoon as we boarded at the Lotto stop, the bus was already full, with no Italian face to be seen. In one section sat a group of heavy-set Russian women, in another a family from Bangladesh or India, and throughout, lots of people speaking Arabic. It was the presence of the later which made us most uneasy. Only several days earlier, in response to the Israeli invasion of southern Lebanon, thousands of Muslims had gathered in Piazzale Loreto to shout anti-Israeli and anti-American slogans. I took off my baseball cap and hoped Hannah and Aidan's caps looked more Italian than American.

Perhaps on account of being extra-vigilant, I noticed when two young men who had been speaking Arabic, stopped and looked in our direction. Had they heard us speaking English? The one facing us would pause from his conversation every so often, then study each of us with intense eyes. I wondered what it was like to look into the face of a genuine terrorist. Just as I was sizing him up, he looked right into my eyes (was I that obvious?).

He reached toward me and, with the back of his hand, tapped me on the shoulder. He had my attention. Then, he brought a finger up to his eye, then dragged it downward, slightly tugging on his cheek: the international sign of caution – look out, be alert, keep your eyes open. *Gulp.* Again, the finger dragged down under his right eye. As if miming the action of pulling on the straps of an imaginary backpack he was carrying, he pointed to the real one I was carrying. Then he jerked his head ever so slightly towards a figure standing behind me.

Once I had understood his silent warning, I switched the pack to my other shoulder. Turning slightly, I noticed the figure behind me back away. I turned back to face the Arab man. He winked and nodded. And suddenly the bus felt slightly less foreign.

Coming Together, as Guests and Hosts

"Let mutual love continue.
Do not neglect to show hospitality to strangers, for by doing that
some have entertained angels without knowing it."

Hebrews 13:1-2

My native language is rather poor when it comes to the word *stranger*. Italian, I am discovering, has several different words for that single word in English: *il forestiere, lo straniero, lo strano, l'extracomunitario* (the traveller, the stranger, the one from outside the community). With so many new Italian words to learn, I was relieved to find out that, at least in one case, the Italians have only one word that requires two in English. The word is *ospite*, which in English can mean both *guest* and *host*.

However, the word *ospite* presents us English-speakers with some confusion. How can we make the distinction between talking about the *host* (the one who sits behind the registration desk, the one who hangs up your coat as you enter the apartment, the one who is busy in the kitchen as the others sit at the dining room table) and the *guest* (the one who rings the bell and waits for the door to be opened, the one who wonders if the little spoon is used for the salad or the dessert, the one who needs direction in finding the bathroom)? After all, don't we need a word that distinguishes the one who *gives* hospitality from the one who *receives* hospitality?

The writer of Hebrews suggests that, perhaps, when followers of Jesus show true hospitality there should be such confusion. In the Body of Christ, it should be difficult to know in which direction the hospitality is flowing. No hosts. No guests. Only *ospiti*.

Furthermore, we Christians trust that when such hospitality is being done, outer identities fade, and inner, more holy ones are revealed. "An unknown guest," John Wesley once wrote about the Hebrews 13 text, "even now [may] be of more worth than he appears."(1) As the church, we people of different tongues and different cultures are, most importantly, people of one Book, which is full of stories of people from outside the community. In those stories we find that the stranger is often someone else in disguise: a fellow traveler, an angel – even Jesus himself.

"… take care to keep open house."

Hebrews 13:2 (*The Bible in Basic English*)

"Why do they not integrate?" asked the Italian woman. She seemed to be expressing some of the exasperation of her compatriots, gathered at this ecumenical gathering to discuss multicultural churches. "They stick to themselves. They do things only with their own nationality group. We ask them to join us, and then they don't come."

Another woman, not Italian, tried to respond. "But, *mia sorella* (my sister), when have you asked me like you really mean it? Sometimes I feel like if you extend an invitation to me, you're only soothing your own conscience. Do you really mean it? Do you really want me in? What would you do if all my friends came in, too? You'd have to start changing the way you do things."

"Of course we want you in, *cara* (dear one). But if you want to be members, you need to take on the responsibilities of members. You can't just expect us to make decisions. You can't expect us to carry all the responsibilities. We're not getting any younger, and the church has bills to pay, responsibilities to keep, decisions to make. You can't just come for worship, then leave when we have to do business."

"Would you let us? You do all your business in a language that is not my strong language. You talk about things that are not familiar to those of us who started coming in the last few years. You have certain ways of doing things that probably don't intend to exclude people like me, but they do. Like scheduling meetings when I'm still at work, or charging money for church suppers that my family can't afford. You may think that you have removed all the barriers, but there are ones still there."

The discussion continued like this for a while. Hard to know if the candid discussions were bearing fruit or just making existing tensions worse.

Arriving home a few hours later, exhausted, I realized I'd forgotten my apartment key. I knocked on the door. A familiar scamper of footsteps ran down the hall, then fumbled with the lock.

"Wait," said the voice, with a hint of mischief, "What's the password?"

"Hmmm… Piggly Wiggly?"

"Wrong," came the answer, "try again."

"Uhhh… how about 'Luke, I am your father'?"

"No, Darth Vader. You're not right."

"Oh wait, I know. It's 'Alexander Beshmirtnik'."

"Who?"

"Alexander Beshmirtnik!"

"No, it's not that!"

"How about, 'I'm hungry and I'm standing out here, and I want to eat my supper!?'"

A slight hesitation ensued, during which the level of frustration in my voice was probably being evaluated. Then, with several twists of the keys, the door finally opened.

The whole afternoon, it seemed, had been spent dealing with doors and locks and keys.

Who's on the inside with the keys? Who's on the outside, wondering how long to wait for the deadbolt to turn? What are the unintentional passwords we use? Have we forgotten that the code to the combination lock may have been shared so long ago that others don't know it? Should the newcomer prove himself trustworthy to be given a key? What would convince both sides to begin removing the locks and the keys – moving towards the honour system?

The teams of bocce men
stand in fours.
Complete units,
selected long ago.
Those who receive,
banter about distance,
and strategy.
Those who roll,
stare down the runway,
intent on spin
or block.
Rules are not posted,
but have been internalized
by some ancient catechesis,
left to the onlooker
to decipher.
Others may watch,
(from behind the fence)
to appreciate technique,
but not interfere –
entrance to the pitch
is restricted.
Not unfriendly,
these greying teammates;
one greets a teammate's wife,
another tussles a grandchild's hair.
But when the rite resumes,
all goes silent –
locked stare,
silent survey
of the angles.
The spheres connect,
then repel.
May I play?
Maybe someday, young man.
And he rests his hand
on the gate.

*"So gather around, come on in, all you refugees
and castoffs."*

Isaiah 45:20 (The Message)

"God told me to do it," she said, from behind the counter. It's not a phrase often heard while ordering Chinese take-out. Was she refusing to hold the MSG? Was she adding some egg rolls to our order? Her pronunciation of Italian is as hard for me to understand as mine is to hers. I asked her to repeat what she had said.

"The Lord told me to use this place," she said, motioning to the twelve tables.

The *Isola Cucina Cinese* is something of an unofficial hang-out for foreigners. Tonight, two Congolese men drink coffee at the counter. A Filippino couple talk over a plate of rice noodles. A group of Moroccan men from the nearby market sit under the fake palm tree in the corner. Several Equadorian transsexuals who have somehow found this a place of refuge sit at another table. And then there's the American family in search of a cheap meal that everyone in the family likes.

Other proprietors would not stand for loitering. But she lets some guests sit without ordering a thing. Since it opens earlier than the Italian restaurants, we often see persons entering as early as five-thirty or six o'clock. She sometimes opens the doors earlier when it is cold outside. Some guests sit long after they've finished their meal and watch the television, or stare at the fish in the tank. No one is allowed to smoke, but we've never seen her chase anyone out.

The owner's Italian is very good and she seems to offer a point of entry to recent immigrants from China. There are always new waiters and waitresses whenever we go in. She is an active member of a Chinese Christian congregation several blocks away, and always asks how things are going at the Chiesa Metodista.

"This Sunday," she said, "after I get back from my own church, this place will be filled with South Americans. A whole congregation. God told me to open my restaurant to them."

"Do you speak Spanish?" I asked, for lack of any clearer question.

"No, I wish I did. We Chinese and the South Americans do not get together very much. What a shame that is. But on Sunday we will cook food for them – we won't charge them a lot. They have their own preacher. He will preach and offer Christ. They can use this place like a church that day. That's what God said to me: offer a place. Will you pray, pastor? Will you pray that God will bless my restaurant?"

"Which one of you, having a hundred sheep and losing one of them, does not leave the other ninety-nine in the wilderness and go after the one that is lost until he finds it?"

Luke 15:4

Two attendants threw ropes over tall poles as the captain manoeuvred the ferry carefully towards the dock. About one-half of the boat's 270 chairs were occupied on this winter morning: tourists, lake commuters, construction workers, island residents bringing groceries back from the mainland. On shore a young attendant left his heated cabin and waited to push the gangplank across the watery gap. As soon as he had the bridge in place, he motioned to the only passenger preparing to disembark – an elderly woman carrying two shopping bags – to come ashore.

After she was safely on land, with a rattle of metal on the stone dock, the dock attendant pulled the gangplank back onto shore. The captain gunned the engines and the water beneath began to churn. With help from the attendant, the crew flipped the thick ropes off the poles and hauled them back in. They exchanged waves, and the attendant walked back towards his warm cubicle.

With the ferry about twenty feet away from the dock, the harbour suddenly echoed with two blasts from its horn. The attendant turned around and looked out inquisitively towards the captain's deck. The captain stuck his arm out the window, waving to the attendant to come back to the edge of the water. The ferry stopped its momentum, briefly trod water, then slowly re-approached the dock.

One of the boat's crew climbed over the ship's guard rail, gripped it tightly with one hand and leaned out towards shore. Meanwhile, with his left arm wrapped around one of the mooring poles, the attendant stretched his right hand out over the water. Reaching out, the crewman passed two black leather gloves across the water. The attendant smiled, pulled himself back to safety and raised them triumphantly in his fist.

By now the old woman with the grocery bags had returned to the dock. The attendant turned, and with both hands reaching out as if extending them on a silver platter, handed the gloves to the woman. With an embarrassed grin and a grateful sigh, the woman took them and gave a sheepish wave to the passengers. Then she looked up in the direction of the Good Captain, and shouted: *"Grazie!! Grazie!!"*

"How to make an effective home visit:
Rule #3: Clarify the reason for your visit."

The Unofficial United Methodist Handbook for Pastors (2)

"Pastor, you are very welcome here," Livingston motioned to the chair near the window in the small kitchen. His voice sounded like a whole bass section.

A small calendar with the black star of the Ghanaian flag sat atop a nearby cabinet.

Elizabeth, his wife, entered the room and smiled. "We are happy to have you here in our home, Pastor." She opened the refrigerator and brought out two plastic bottles. Then, wheeling around, she held them both up for me to see. "Which would you like, Pastor? There is orange and there is water."

"Water would be fine," I responded.

Replacing the bottle of soda back in the refrigerator, she nimbly took two glasses with her free hand and placed them on the counter. Then she reached below the kitchen table, removed a short stool with a circular top, and placed it between me and her husband. Opening a drawer, she took out a yellow cloth placemat and draped it over the stool in front of me. She returned to the counter, poured water in each glass and brought the two full glasses and placed them on the stool. "Ah, you are welcome."

I took a sip of the water. Livingston boomed, "Now Pastor, tell us why you have come." Caught a little off-balance by the directness of his question, I tried to explain that I was here just on a social call, to get to know them a bit better, blah, blah, blah … and that there was no problem I wished to discuss, blah, blah, blah …" They both laughed, good-naturedly. I gave them a quizzical look.

"You see, Pastor," Livingston explained, "in our country, when a guest comes to call, the first thing we do is we pour water for them. They have come a long way and their journey has been hard. We say, *"Akwaaba"* – this means 'You are welcome very here'."

"The second thing we do is we ask them a very important question. We say, "You have come a long way to see us. What is your purpose of coming?"

*"He said to them, "Take nothing for your journey,
no staff, nor bag, nor bread, nor money – not even an extra tunic.*

Luke 9:3-4

These words, uttered by the same teacher who waved off material concerns such as *What will we eat?* or *What will we drink?* (Matthew 6:31), would not have put my traveller's mind at ease. Take nothing with you: no backpack, no money, no extra shirt, no hand soap, no water bottle. Oh, and no sandwiches or snacks either.

We get excited when visitors from home bring us gifts of food: maple syrup, cornbread mix, peanut butter, Skyline chili. Sometimes they even leave the rest of their *gorp* (good old raisins and peanuts) mix that they had packed for their journey. It is unthinkable that any of us would leave home without a taste of home accompanying us. So, what was Jesus getting at?

He sent them out to depend on other peoples' hospitality, to sit at other peoples' tables, to eat from other peoples' plates, to be served other peoples' cuisine. Part of the marching orders for mission, it seemed, was to live on someone else's terms: 'radical hospitality' turned on its head.

At a recent anti-immigrant rally in Milano, a demonstrator carried a placard which read, *Si alla Polenta. No al Couscous* (Yes to Polenta, No to Couscous)(3). Polenta, a boiled corn meal, is a traditional dish native to the north of Italy. Couscous, tiny balls of pasta made from two different kinds of flour with Middle-eastern and North African origins, is found in a growing number of Moroccan and Algerian grocery stores around Milano.

A famous chef once commented, "There are few things more personal than eating, and if you reject someone's food, you kind of reject them."(4) I suppose the inverse would be true, too. If you accept someone's food, you kind of accept them.

Before he sent the disciples out empty-handed, Jesus reminded them of their primary mission; and it had a lot to do with acceptance.

*"Instead, by speaking the truth in a spirit of love,
we must grow up in every way to Christ, who is the head."*

Ephesians 4:15 (Good News Bible)

You really had to hand it to this Sunday school class. Italian, African, Asian, they had been asked to come up with a list of words that describe the word *accoglienza* (welcome). It's the same Italian word given to the person who hands out bulletins and hymnals at the door of sanctuary, but they quickly got past that. In red, green and blue markers on the erasable easel, they brainstormed some 36 words, like *accettare* (to accept someone), *concordanza* (agreement), *appoggiare* (to support), *aiuto* (help), *amicizia* (friendship).

An 18-year-old slammed his hand on his knee. "Wait a minute," he said, "I know this discussion is getting all nice and Christian and stuff. But what am I supposed to do when it was a Moldovian guy who beat up my friend?"

Or consider one of the church elders. He certainly could not be accused of offering a reluctant welcome to foreigners in the congregation. He has opened his home, given concrete assistance, and does volunteer work with immigrants. In any discussions about integration of the church, he's got *street cred*. On a recent drive through Chinatown, an area simmering with recent tensions about parking ordinances for merchants, he commented, "They're welcome to move here and to set up their shops. But then they want to have special laws about parking their trucks? Separate laws for separate parts of the city? I'm all for respect," he said as his face got redder, "but you live in *our* city; you live by *our* rules!"

Or a pastor at the forefront of the intercultural movement. She has risked the ire of her congregation by opening the doors of the church to the large Nigerian, Cameroonian and Ghanaian communities in her city. The council even gave them permission to have prayer time in their own language and style, complete with a key to the church. As she sat with her pastoral colleagues one day, she chuckled as she recounted a recent event.

"It was midnight and downstairs in the church they were all still singing and dancing with their drums and tambourines. Our apartment is right above all this, not to mention all the neighbouring apartments. I said to my husband, 'Can you go down and talk with them? If I go downstairs, I'm likely to explode'."

After ten years of seeking to *essere la chiesa insieme* (be the church together), some Italian Methodists are finding that their openness has its limits. Some initial exuberance has given way to disappointment. Some outstretched arms have been retracted. Some idealism (to quote a political theorist) has been mugged by certain realities. Platitudes of faith language built on the sand don't last the rainy season. Magic marker jottings on a white board erase easily. Christian *accoglienza* is a gritty business – anger, frustration, miscommunication, constant negotiation, repeated dialogue. It's no wonder those young people included other words in their list: *forgiveness, challenge, honesty, reaching agreement, cou*rage.

Why would anything – including providing welcome – taught by a man who talked about the cross, be easy? In his church, it's more than just handing out hymnals.

"Do not let the foreigner joined to the Lord say,
"The Lord will surely separate me from his people";…
For my house shall be called a house of prayer for all peoples."

Isaiah 56:3-7

When you refer to me and my friends as "the immigrants," should we refer to you as "the natives"? In church we should be able to find better words than that.

I know that the names of my family are hard for you to pronounce. Some of yours aren't easy either. That day you addressed my daughter by name, it honoured our entire family.

Do you know that to us, many of you Europeans also look alike? Perhaps we will have to study one another's faces a little closer.

It is true that I am without work. I appreciate your wanting to help, but it embarrasses me a little, too. Understand if my appreciation is a little understated.

Don't worry if, from time to time, I want to relax in a corner of the fellowship hall with friends from my own culture. It is not a sign of separation.

When we hand out jobs to be done at church, I really want to help. Please remember though, that I mop floors all week. I am willing to mop at church, too – just not all the time.

You don't speak any of my languages. I have worked hard to learn yours. Please be patient, even in an important meeting, even if we are pressed for time, if my words don't come out freely.

You have all lived with one another a long time. You have plenty of stories to tell and memories that you share. But after a while, you may notice that I become silent.

By the way, don't take my silence for ignorance. Sometimes it is me respecting you, or listening to you, or holding my ideas for another time.

Do you remember the time at that church activity when I looked so confused, and you turned to me and explained what was going on? I appreciated that.

Some day I hope you will come to my country. There we treat the guest like a king, like a queen. That is how we would welcome you.

Thank you for opening the doors of this church – this 'house of prayer for all peoples' – to me. I realize that this was your congregation long before I arrived. Now I am here, and I look forward to being less a guest and more a brother.

"O God, enlarge my heart, that it may be big enough to receive the greatness of your love.
Stretch my heart, that it may take into it all those around the world who believe in Jesus.
Swell my heart, that it may take in all those who are not lovely in my eyes, and whose hands I do not want to touch. Amen."

A prayer from South Africa

For decades the grounds of the convent have stretched across the meadow and somewhere into the distant woods. For years, villagers have hiked across that expanse to attend morning prayer at the house of the Missionarie di Maria Saveriane. The sisters are known for their hospitality and care for the poor, far beyond the reaches of their property line.

Some of the sisters have been distressed lately at the encroaching construction. Each year, it seems, the condominiums of the nearby town get closer and closer. Little by little, the forest is disappearing. The horizon has more concrete on it than it ever had before. Noise from the approaching town has even entered the cloistered world of the convent.

Not long ago, the mother superior of the order came to visit. Her last visit had been some years ago, when the community enjoyed more seclusion. She looked out a window across the field. "Oh my," she said, "things have certainly changed around here. Look how our family has grown."

Together, on the Same Soil

"Woman, believe me, the hour is coming when you will worship the Father neither on this mountain nor in Jerusalem."

John 4:21

The craggy knob of the Castelluzzo is visible from any point in the historic Waldensian town of Torre Pellice. The parking lot of the Waldensian guest house offers a clear view of the mountain. From the grassy front lawn of Torre Pellice's Waldensian Church, the mountain top seems to poke through the forest of pine trees. On a plaster model of the Val Pellice (Pellice valley) that sits in the foyer of the Waldensian history museum, the Castelluzzo is labelled, complete with elevation of 1,004 metres. The Waldensians claim it as part of their landscape.

According to historical accounts, during various chapters in the Waldensians' tragic history, the rock had served as a refuge. It contains a cavern, called the *Bars d'la Tajola*, that one guidebook states, had "preserved many hundreds of people from the last horrors of cruelty". For as many as three weeks at a time, the cave held up to 400 people seeking shelter from anti-Protestant purges.

It's a two-hour hike to the top. With each step up the incline, it is not hard to imagine the Waldensian forefathers and mothers who made the trek years ago. With a Waldensian guidebook in hand, the walkway provides vantage points from which to see other Waldensian landmarks: the Waldensian Hall, site of the annual Waldensian-Methodist Synod; the Waldensian Hospital; the farm of Waldensian leader Henry Arnaud. The path feels like a Waldensian heritage trail.

After some time at the summit, I turned to make my way back down the mountain.

Perched above the Waldensian cave was a large boulder. On it, a plaque was bolted into the rock. Fully expecting another Waldensian marker, it was a bit of a shock to read it. No mention of the Waldensians at all. It commemorates the Church of Jesus Christ of Latter-Day Saints, when in 1850, an Elder Lorenzo Snow and other elders met there to launch mission work in this valley and into Switzerland. They had renamed the place 'The Rock of Prophesy', and its taller neighbour, *Vandalino*, they renamed 'Mount Brigham'. The Mormons? What were they doing here? Isn't this a *Waldensian* Valley?

There are so many layers to the lands we religious groups call *holy*. The Jews' Temple Mount is also the site of the Muslims' Al-Aqsa Mosque. The town of Cana, in which Jesus visited a wedding, was ground zero last week to an Israeli attack in Lebanon. One people's holy land is another's trail of tears. One's *Bars d'la Tajola* is another's Rock of Prophesy.

God created the Earth, and a saw that it was good. And then people have tussled over patches of it for years, with claims that God had ordained it for *them*. Compared to looking up at it from below, the view of Castelluzzo must be very different – from heaven.

*"Accept Your people, O Lord our God, and receive their prayer.
Restore the most holy service of your house…"*

(English translation of part of the *Shemoneh Esrei*,
a prayer of the synagogue)

The synagogue on Via Farini in Florence is thought to be one of the most beautiful Jewish places of worship in the world. Constructed between 1874 and 1882, the building's green domes are visible on city's famous skyline. Along the horizon and from up close, it could even pass for a Catholic or Orthodox church. That is no accident.

"You might notice," said the young woman who showed us around inside, "that there are some things here that are not usually in a *shul* (synagogue)." She pointed to the pipe organ at the front of the sanctuary and then over to a tall, rather Catholic-looking pulpit on the side. "We do not really use those things," she said with a slight smile. "Maybe you would ask, why are they here? Well, it is because the two architects who designed this building were not even Jewish. They were Christians.

"When you are surrounded by a Christian culture, you do some things to look more like the culture around you. Perhaps, back then, the members of our community were trying to show that they were not so different from the society.

"Still, some Jewish people who visit become quite upset when they see it for the first time. For me it is not such a problem. After all, in our tradition, it is not so important – the place. Over time, this congregation has had to learn that the building and what's in the building *is* important, but it is not *the* most important thing."

The history of this temple bears out her observation. First, the racial laws instituted by the Fascist government in 1938 made it difficult for people to worship here freely. When the occupation of Italy came, Nazi soldiers used the synagogue as a place to store goods confiscated from Jewish homes. Later, before they retreated north to escape the Allied invasion from the south, German troops mined the building. Only some quick-thinking Italian partisans, who defused the explosive devices, saved it from total destruction.

Later, after the repeal of the Italian racial laws in 1943, the congregation held its meeting in the gardens adjacent to the synagogue. After the liberation, the community observed its first Rosh Hashanah in a local theatre.

"We have come to learn that we can worship God in any place – that any room can be a *sinagoga*. All you need is an altar, the Ark, and at least one of the scrolls of the Torah. And, of course, the people. Yes, the people. And there you have the holy place."

"Assemble yourselves and come together,
draw near, you survivors of the nations!"

Isaiah 45:20

The driver of the hearse would surely have needed directions to find this place. The city pavement runs out a kilometer or so back. Tucked far behind the wall of the pipe factory, the hearse was the only four-wheeled vehicle in sight. The dirt path, lined with trash and peppered with pot-holes, glistened from the light rain. Three old bicycles leaned against dirty mattress. Seven or eight trailers, balanced on two wheels and cinder blocks lined the gravel courtyard. The homes of the homeless.

A tarpaulin had been strung between two trees, tied taut with military precision. A plastic-metallic crucifix hung from the back of the cloth. Underneath, a rough-wood coffin sat on a simple table. Bouquets of chrysanthemums rested on either side of the makeshift tent. Baskets of flowers lined an imaginary path by which the mourners could approach.

The driver, the only man in a jacket and tie, smoked nervously near the hearse, occasionally glancing at his watch. The mourners gathered under the canopy, talking. One African woman had her arm around a little girl. Two men who appeared to be Roma, swatted some pigeons off the tarp. Another woman, also a Roma, smoothed out the rug which had been placed at the foot of the coffin.

Far from any church or funeral home, this clearing in the trees had become something of a temple, a sanctuary for this departed soul and his nomadic community: these 'survivors of the nations' – a community.

"On that day there will be an altar to the Lord
in the centre of the land...,
and a pillar to the Lord at its border."

Isaiah 19:19

On the third Sunday of July each year, two congregations, one from the French village of Abries, the other from the Italian region of Val Pellice, meet to worship together on a mountaintop. There are no roads which connect their two towns. In fact, the members of the two communities probably do not see one another, except at this annual event. For the rest of the year they sit in deep valleys on opposite sides of the mountains. When one is in shadow, the other is in light.

Some level of negotiation goes into planning the event each year. Presumably, before the villages were connected by phone lines, the planning was done by hearty messengers, strong on energy and endurance. Surely they would have been gifted barrier-crossers, capable enough in the other's tongue to negotiate details of time, place and supplies.

Even today, while the congregational leaders can talk logistics on their cell phones, they still must be careful in their preparation. Both groups need enough time to make the hike of several hours up the mountain. Both need to allow ample time to descend the mountain by nightfall. Who will bring the chalice? For communion – your bread or ours? What will it be this year – Bordeaux or Chianti? If your members can bring their own hymnbooks, we'll do the same. No one's backpack should be unduly burdened.

Worship itself reflects the blend of cultures. Some hymns in Italian, others in French. Liturgy combines words of both. Texts are shared beforehand so that sermons may be on the same theme. Bilingual worship leaders try to include all who have gathered. Afterwards, people share their lunches – "Have you ever tried this dish?" "Well no…" "…and here's a delicacy from our village for you to sample."

Before descending the respective sides of the mountain, they do some preliminary planning for next year's meeting. If the trek was farther for one congregation last year, a point closer to the other congregation will be chosen this year. (Last year, the Italians joked to their French friends that their ascent was at least twice as long.)

The particular mountain, however, is not in question. Worship is on the same peak each year. It is called *Colla della Croce* (Hill of the Cross). What better place for worshipping at the border?

Together, in the City

"Then, because so many people were coming and going that they did not even have a chance to eat, he said to them, 'Come with me by yourselves to a quiet place…'."

Mark 6:31 NIV

What a noisy place, the city. The trams stop clattering down our street shortly after 1:00am, and resume at 5:00am. The restaurants around the corner don't close until after midnight. Outside our windows, people shout. Before sunrise each Wednesday, the recycling truck starts its route under our window; all the wine bottles from the previous week smash into its metal belly. Doors slam. Ambulances wail. All around the neighbourhood, spoons stir cappuccinos with a ching-ching-ching like an early morning bell choir concert. City dwellers in any part of the world learn to cope, hopefully learning over time how to make background static of it all.

But what of our spiritual lives in the city? Those of us who were taught that the spirit comes in silence, in the still small voices, in the peaceful times and places, are faced with a real challenge in the city.

While living in Rome, the author Henri Nouwen observed all the congestion, the noise, the smells, the movement of the city. In the midst of everything, he noted that:

…there are the domes of Rome pointing to the places set apart of the Holy One. The churches of Rome are like beautiful frames around empty spaces witnessing to Him who is the quiet still centre of all human life… They want to invite us to be silent, to sit or kneel, to listen attentively, and to rest with our whole being.(1)

That kind of rest, that kind of 'still centre' is most difficult in the city. I recently heard a Waldensian pastor preach on the Second Corinthians distinction between our 'outer nature' and our 'inner nature' (4:16). In a notably Protestant take on Nouwen's Roman Catholic imagery, he drew our attention to the landscape of the city as mirroring our spiritual lives. A city like Milano, he said, threatens to overwhelm us with its noise and pace. It represents our outer nature. But squeezed between the condominiums and office buildings are places of green. The parks, like our inner being, are places of renewal and seclusion.

My mind began conjuring up images of parks we have visited. All of them, however, are *outside* the city limits, long bus rides away. As if intuiting my unintentional drift, the preacher reminded us that he was talking of parks *within* the city limits. Yes, there are places of green, however small, in the concrete jungle of the city.

The image was clear: escaping the city does not always bring peace. There are places of peace, even holiness, within it and within us. God of nature, God of the Church, help me to see the tree, the dome, as an invitation – not to leave or vacate, but to enter *a quiet place*.

"Ever since the creation of the world, his eternal power
and divine nature, invisible though they are,
have been understood and seen through the things he has made"

Romans 1:20

We rarely hear the sound of birds –
not enough trees;
tyres screech, trams rumble, car alarms wail,
but not many signs of nature in the city.
Piazza pigeons, a rat on the subway tracks –
they are the extent of Gotham wildlife…
but for this tree in our courtyard,
which, in some solitary defiance,
has endured a battle with smog,
and asphalt encroachment.
It looks down on the road department depot
and the church beside it.
With no other green companion in sight,
this one has not given up
doing what comes naturally:
it blossoms, gives shade, shivers in a breeze,
and when fall comes, it releases its leaves.
on our church.
A nuisance, say some –
wet leaves cause rot, you know,
sending water to trickle through the roof
of our underground sanctuary.
So, our little squad of dominion
is out here today,
brooms in hand
(no rakes – they are more rural fare).
The rustic smell,
the yellows and reds showered
across these drab concrete slabs,
feel like a divine reclamation,
a quiet reminder
that neither exhaust nor sidewalks
nor iron gates, nor anything else
in this urban creation,
has been able to separate us,
from an eternal cycle.

> *"There will always be poor people in the land.*
> *Therefore, I command you to be open-handed*
> *towards your brothers*
> *and toward the poor and needy in your land"*

Deuteronomy 15:11 (NIV)

More often than not, followed by the closing of the subway doors, we hear the beginning of a familiar monologue, *"Signore e signori, scusate che vi disturbo. Sono una madre povera..."* ("Ladies and gentleman, please excuse me for disturbing you. I am a poor mother...") She is typically carrying a small child on her hip and a crumpled paper cup in the other hand. On other metro rides, a group of men sing to an accordion and guitar, then walk around with an half-open canvas sack for donations. Most people bury their faces in their newspapers.

People who beg for money are all over Milano. Outside the banks, "Morning, boss, would you consider a gift?" At the intersections, "Please signora, can I wash your windshield?" As the automatic doors of grocery stores open onto the street, outstretched hands and imploring faces. At the ticket window of the movie theatre, *"Ciao, mio fratello, do you want to buy one of these books?"* Diners in restaurants are often accosted by men carrying bunches of flowers and an instamatic camera; they approach each table, soliciting couples to buy a rose or have a photo taken. Persons entering and leaving churches often need to walk past someone seated on a flattened cardboard box, asking for some change.

We live in the same building as the church; our doorbell rings several times a week with requests. Could you pay for a bus ticket back to Poland? I just need the money to pay for my permit to stay. My employer refused to pay me and I just need some money to get me to the first of the month. Can you help?

There is a relentlessness to the requests, a cycle to the needs, an endlessness to the suffering. It is hard not to feel bombarded, even used. Jesus acknowledged that poor people and poverty will not go away. Yet, just as in Deuteronomy, the assessment challenges us to choose: hard-hearted fatigue or new wells of compassion.

God, give me grace not to see a mass of people, but individuals. Do not allow me to become close-handed.

*"…the prostitutes are going into the kingdom of God
ahead of you…"*

Matthew 21:31

*Her steady stare
from the driver seat
of the idling Renault
follows me
as I walk past
on the sidewalk.
Her heavy eyelashes
do not blink.
The rouge mask
cannot hide her tired eyes
or severe countenance.
Anger or enticement?
Her enamelled lips
purse, then open slightly,
causing a slight ripple
under her chin.
Her hand slowly drops,
rests on her thigh,
varicosed in blue;
Her woollen sweater
is unbuttoned;
her cleavage wrinkled with age;
too much skin
for this February morning.
She will be passed by
for more lithe prospects
who wait down the block.*

How long has the engine
been running,
the heat on –
hours…years?
I quicken my step,
not sure what
unsettles me more:
that our eyes had met…
or that
the man from Nazareth
was criticized for
spending time
with the likes of her.

"...and on the seventh day..."

Genesis 2:2

...the parish priest of Pianura had had enough. For the past six days he and his parishioners had watched the bags of trash pile up in their neighbourhood in Napoli. Because of a complex impasse between government officials, the garbage collectors union, and the ubiquitous influence of the Camorra (an organized crime network in Naples), trash has gone uncollected for a week. Bags stuffed with Christmas wrapping, stale pieces of holiday *panettone*, and New Year's lentils piled higher and higher. Newspapers blared the headlines, *Emergenza Rifiuti* (Garbage Emergency).

Rats raced from street corner to street corner. Parents kept their children inside for fear of disease. Angry citizens had begun setting fires to mountains of trash. City politicians launched partisan attacks on one another. The Prime Minister dispatched the military to Napoli to assure the reopening of schools after the winter break. A summit was called with local officials and the Ministers of the Environment and Defence to resolve the crisis.

On Epiphany Sunday, with tons of trash still uncollected, Don Giuseppe took his parishioners to the streets. In his white clerical alb, he led a procession of some 4,000 people toward the city dump. Some carried banners. Children shouted "No dumping! No disease!" Standing in front of a makeshift altar and holding a microphone, he began the mass near the trash. Unlike the usual pillars and icons of his church, behind him loomed six overflowing dumpsters and a bulldozed hill of earth, speckled with bulging yellow and white plastic bags.

He called on city officials to come to the negotiating table. He called for the reopening of the schools. He called on all who would collabourate with the Camorra to see the benefits of putting thousands of garbage collectors back to work. "Brothers and sisters," he shouted into the microphone, "we are not trash!"

And then, as he does at every mass, lifted the cup high, and blessed the bread, and professed the presence of the Lord in the Eucharist, even in this place.

*"There is no faithfulness or loyalty,
and no knowledge of God in the land."*

Hosea 4:1

Film critics have noted that Italian cinema often paints Italian life with sweeping comedic strokes or nostalgic looks at bucolic country life. That makes a recent release like *A Casa Nostra* all the more controversial. Set in Milano, the film is a dark portrayal of modern life in Italy's financial capital. Scandals, corruption, violence, infidelity, dishonesty – so bleak a picture that Milano's mayor lodged a formal complaint that the film had inaccurately depicted her city.

A Casa Nostra's Milano shows models who are addicted to drugs, lost men whose only intimacy can be found with prostitutes, immigrants who can only make money through prostitution, bankers who banter over soccer during lunch and plot illegal acquisitions before dinner, and couples who lead separate lives of deceit. Bankrupt souls move with no guiding principles higher than a brief moment of pleasure or a quick Euro. Power is wielded for personal gain. Greed is unchecked. Grief is unattended. Honest conversations are avoided. These are not the images the city's Chamber of Commerce puts on its brochures.

Only in retrospect did we realize that some things do not appear in the film. There are very few smiles. There are almost no children. Other than a quick scene of a mass at a Romanian Orthodox Church (with a cameo appearance by one of our colleagues on the Christian council), there are no signs of an effectual religious presence. The Duomo, typically revered as the heart of the city, is shown once, at dawn: silent, closed, and partially obscured by scaffolding. This is a society, which according to the film's director Francesca Comencini, has "misplaced its moral compass."

The morning after we'd seen the film it was difficult to get motivated for ministry; as if the scenes of depravity and desolation were too close to some of our own observations. Who do we think we are, this Christian community tucked in a little neighbourhood in this mess of a city? How does the church stand a chance against decades of ethical decay, rampant capitalism, unchecked hedonism? Church work can feel like trying to empty an ocean with a spoon. The morning's indictment by Hosea (a prophet whose own setting could hardly be described as comedic or bucolic) of the eighth century BC. Israel sounded strangely similar to the film's critique of twenty-first century Italy: *"Swearing, lying, and murder, and stealing and adultery break out; bloodshed follows bloodshed."*(4:2)

Hosea and Ms. Comencini seemed to be about the same task. They both describe the situation of a people. They both try to unmask the reality. They both condemn what they see. In the clamor caused by *A Casa Nostra*, one commentator came to the director's defence, saying that her social criticism was "An act of love for the city [by] telling things as they are." (2)

Hosea, however, would take that act of love a step further, invoking a God who stares straight into the depravity and says, *"How can I give you up, Ephraim? How can I hand you over, O Israel? ...My heart recoils within me; my compassion grows warm and tender..."* (11:8)

"O come, thou Dayspring, come and cheer
our spirits by thy justice here;
disperse the gloomy clouds of night,
and death's dark shadows put to flight."(3)

The small park behind the church of Santa Maria della Fontana is still almost dark. December hoarfrost coats the benches and the asphalt beneath them is black with a thin coat of ice. Hints of sunlight bounce off the blue and black graffiti covering the glistening concrete wall. Black smoke billows up from a small bonfire on the pavement.

A few metres behind the park benches, on the other side of a wrought-iron fence, the morning frost still coats the grass. Each balcony of the condominium is draped with strands of identical blinking lights. Furnace smoke wafts out of the chimney atop the sixth floor. The evergreen tree in the courtyard is decorated with colourful lights that, presumably, have been left on all night.

A man with a woollen hat and a drab, brown overcoat scavenges the black pavement for pieces of newspaper and twigs, then tosses them into the fire. He rubs his palms together, holding them towards the flames.

A man in a coat and cashmere scarf emerges from the apartment building, jingles his keys and disappears into the cavernous car-park beneath. He cups his hands near his mouth, takes a pair of leather gloves out of his jacket pocket and slips them on.

The fire consumes a corrugated box and two sticks, sending sparks heavenward.

The lights on the Christmas tree morph from green to red, then begin to blink.

The man in the brown coat, his back to the fence, tucks his hands under his armpits. The fire begins to sputter. He gives the glowing branch a kick with his shoe.

The man with the scarf, his back to the fence, takes off his outer jacket, smoothes it out and drapes it across the back seat of the car. He aims a remote at the garage door.

The first man, now slumped on one of the benches, reaches for a bag, gets up and begins shuffling towards the street. A little pile of grey ashes releases one last trickle of smoke.

The other man slams his car door shut. In a cough of exhaust, the car leaves the driveway and the massive automated gates thunder shut behind it. The lights on the Christmas tree keep on blinking.

"The voice of one crying out in the wilderness…"

Matthew 3:3

The Dalai Lama was in town. He was offering an afternoon talk at the basketball arena on the east side of the city. The only problem with getting there was that this was the second Sunday of December. Stores were open for the Sant'Ambrogio holiday weekend. Some 400 outdoor booths were set up at the annual *Oh Bey, Oh Bey* open-air market outside the city's Castello Sforzesco, offering everything from Japanese body lotion to African mahogany furniture to Bob Marley T-shirts. A few blocks away, the annual *Fiera Artigianale* was wrapping up its nine-day run at the convention centre; eight mammoth pavillions filled with German bratwurst stands, Sicilian pottery dealers, and Indian incense parlours. Christmas commerce was clogging the city's arteries. Anyone wanting to hear *La Sua Santità* from Tibet would have to make an effort to get to him.

At the subway stops vendors hawked faux Louis Vuitton purses and Armani sunglasses. A mother and father searched for a stray mitten at the ticket turnstile ("Take the bags, dear!" he snapped. "I can't," she shot back, "I've got the boys!"). One woman wrestled an unwieldy dried-flower display down the escalator. A man hugged a wrapped canvas painting the size of a surfboard to his chest as he shuffled sideways onto the crowded subway. Five young men wearing blue Inter football scarves, on their way to San Siro stadium for that afternoon's match, sang inebriated choruses. Two women alternated holding their wrists to one another's noses, sniffing department store perfume samples.

The crowds getting off at the arena were no less thick, but noticeably quieter. Ascending the escalators were university students, thirty-something couples, aging hippies, several persons in Buddhist togas, others in orange hats or scarves, some wearing *Free Tibet* T-shirts. Grandparents with grandchildren, teenagers with parents, yuppies with small children: the kind of cross-section that other organized religious groups in these parts can only dream about, were all coming to hear one man speak.

Inside the arena, the famous 72-year-old monk with his trademark smile and glasses, walked onto the platform, placed his hands together in greeting, and nodded to the crowd. After polite applause, people were seated. In the pause that followed as he seemed to centre himself, not a cough, not a sneeze, not a rustle came from any of the 9,000 people in the audience.

For the next two hours the holy man spoke about peace – peace among nations that begins with peace with oneself. His was a gentle but pointed critique of a world he seemed to know thoroughly, but remained outside. "Peace of mind you cannot buy in a store," he said (had he witnessed the scenes outside?) "If you were to go into a shop with 1,000 Euros in your pocket and say to the clerk, 'I would like to purchase peace of mind, he would think you were a crazy person. You cannot buy that." Nods of recognition all around.

This is the day that Christians read about another holy man crying in another wilderness. A crowd came to hear him, too. Who knows what they were after? They were from all walks of life: Pharisees, Sadducees, tax collectors, soldiers and others who followed him into the desert, in search of something they weren't apparently finding in the hustle and bustle of Jerusalem.

"Yet in thy dark streets shineth the everlasting light…"

Phillips Brooks, 1868 (4)

An inner-city sheep, he;
legs formed from cigarettes,
head a bit scuffed.
His companions
in the urban school manger
are a matchstick cow
(with incendiary red hooves)
and a shepherd
(donning the red and black
of AC Milan).
The fourth-grade sculptor
of one wise man,
decided to give him,
instead of myrrh,
a bag
(flea-market Gucci).
Another king is in a boat,
fishing. Fishing?
The angels are not too heavenly,
but perched on a wall,
as if watching a game,
upper tier, last row;
not indifferent,
but not overly present either.
The star is painted in
quick tempera brush-strokes
on corrugated cardboard –
no bigger than a streetlight;
visible, but not
obtrusive.
The Christ child?
Cushioned in
cotton balls
beside the bus depot,
so entirely Emmanuel,
God-with-us,
as to blend in
to the city streets.

"When they saw that the star had stopped,
they were overwhelmed with joy."

Matthew 2:10

Christmas stars, once strung over *Via Borsieri*,
having done their work for a season,
now waited in stacks on the curb.
A screech of tyres, a thud of work boots,
and a team of star-gatherers descended upon each pile.
One by one, each five-pointed frame
was tossed up over the railing
into the gloved hands of another
– as if props in some casual juggling act –
onto the boarded expanse of the flatbed.
These, the signs of Bethlehem and manger,
the guides of kings and shepherds,
these lights which made this dark street shineth,
now unplugged, unlit, and under a tarp,
had blinked their last blink,
presumably 'til next Christmas.
With the yank of the wheel and a puff of exhaust,
they're off to begin their 11-month hibernation.
Only mid-January, this early retirement.
The church calls the season Epiphany – the time of light.
But not here. Lights out, early.
Any twinkle, twinkle from above
will have to work its way
through the winter nights and the smog.
That, and the shafts of neon
from the nearby fruit stand, the jazz club,
the *gelateria* and the pet shop,
will have to suffice.

So job well done, you not-so everlasting lights,
piercing darkness, bringing cheer, and all.
You have brightened a small corner of the kingdom,
your ignoble end befits the one you heralded.
Just knowing that you are nestled in some dusty warehouse,
tucked somewhere behind the plastic pine boughs,
poised to be illuminated next year,
is a small reassurance
of the things hoped for,
some latent promise
of things unseen.

Together, in the Empire

"God...saves those who hope in him"

Daniel, Chapter 13, verse 60, *The New American Bible*

In the Christian catacombs of Priscilla in Rome, the biblical character Daniel figures prominently. Along the underground tunnels which contain some 40,000 ancient tombs, are frescoes which date back to the period between 220-250 AD One shows Daniel, Shadrach and Abednego standing in the furnace. Another shows Daniel facing down a lion. The most intriguing fresco, however, shows Daniel alongside a woman. The Benedictine sister who was leading our small group said, "And you will remember the story of Susanna and Daniel". Kristin and I looked at one another – had we slept through that one in seminary?

The thirteenth chapter of Daniel (for most Protestants the book of Daniel has only twelve), contains the story of Susanna – the beautiful, God-fearing daughter of Joakim and Hilkah. Living in Babylon, her parents had raised her according to the law of Moses. When Susanna was a young woman, two corrupt elders of the people were appointed as judges. One day, they spied Susanna in her garden and they both lusted after her. They demanded that she lie with each of them. If she refused, they threatened to testify against her that she had unlawfully allowed a young man into her garden.

Susanna realized their trap and shrieked for help. When the people of the village came to her aid, the two wicked elders made their accusations against her. The case was taken to a public trial, where Susanna, "through her tears...looked up to heaven, for she trusted in the Lord wholeheartedly". The assembly, however, believed the trumped-up charges of the elders and sentenced Susanna to death. Then, "as she was being led to execution, God stirred up the holy spirit of a young boy named Daniel." He lambasted the members of the assembly for their stupidity, then proceeded to interrogate the two accusers. With Perry Mason precision, he separated the two, found inconsistencies with their stories and exposed their lies. "The whole assembly," the story concludes, "cried aloud, blessing God who saves those who hope in him."

For Christians facing persecution, the guide explained, this story would have brought considerable comfort. In these subterranean places of Christian worship, one only needed to look up through the narrow air shafts to the surface to be reminded of the presence of the Empire. When the powerful hegemony of the Empire threatens your existence as a community, your own narrative is all that is left to give you reassurance and courage. So, you tell the stories that most matter to inspire the faithful to stand up to Caesar – like Daniel unhurt in King Nebuchadnezzar's flames, or Daniel unscathed by King Darius' lions, or Daniel coming to the aid of a woman of faith who faced persecution. You paint the frescoes in your place of worship to remind your children, your grand-children, and – quite unforeseeably – even twenty-first century Christians, that God, often through the messengers God sends, stands on the side of those in peril.

"Blessed are those who are persecuted for righteousness' sake..."

Matthew 5:10

The text for the morning's worship was the Beatitude about persecution. We asked members of the community to name some incidents when they, or someone they know, was subjected to persecution because of their faith in Christ. At first, there was silence. People looked at the ground or up at the ceiling heaters. Nobody seemed too eager to talk about the topic.

Finally, one man broke the ice. "At my work here in Milano," he said, "when I meet other Africans, they assume that because I am black, I am a Moslem. They are all friendly to me. We talk often. One day they ask me, 'You are a Moslem, right?' I say, 'No, I am a Christian. I have been a Christian all my life.' For about six months after that they would not speak to me."

One mother of a teenager raised her hand: "In this city, for young people to say they are Christian is a very strange thing," she said. "In many ways this city has very little religion. It's very secular. So many people in this city think that being a Christian is very strange. Some of her friends have treated her differently because of it. I am just glad that she has some friends who are Christians."

Another man stood up. "In my country," he said, "a Christian butcher sold some pork to a Muslim man in a market. The Muslim man was very angry that he sold him pork. He killed the man. Because of that, there is much fighting between Christians and Muslims."

A young woman from Eastern Europe said, "When I was younger, I began to keep fellowship with a certain group of young Christians in my town. They were doing good work. They were meeting for prayer and studying Bible. I began to do things with that group. My family did not like it. My friends did not like it, too. They thought I was joining a sect. This is how I wanted to be a Christian, but they did not understand. Even when our little group went to the hospital, people would ask us, "Why are you here doing this help?" We would say, "We are doing it because we are Christians," they thought we had other reasons. They did not trust us."

"When I lived in Saudi Arabia," added another woman, "we had to worship with only a small group of people. Really, it was against the law. So we had to do it very quietly. One group would gather in a school class room somewhere. If you were lucky, maybe there would be a priest from time to time. If you were caught, the penalties could be severe. We were often afraid."

"...all you who are weary and carrying heavy burdens..."

Matthew 11:28

One day, during the intercessory prayer time at church, one man came to the altar. In the Philippines he had been an engineer with the government. Here, he works 14 hours a day as a domestic. "I wish to give a testimony," he said quietly. "I had to go the *Questura* (the immigration office) this week". Moaning and sympathetic laughter rose from the congregation. "Yes," he said, "my wife and son and I got on that line at 3:00am. And when we finally got to the window, the woman looked at all our papers.

She said, "You made a mistake. Come back in a month."

"Signora," I said to her, "what did I do wrong? I do not understand."

"Come back in a month!" she said again.

"I did not know how to respond. I said, 'You should not treat me this way!' I was so angry. I could not help it. My wife told me to be more quiet; that I would make things worse for us. But I kept shouting, "I am like you! I am a human being! Treat me like a human being!"

He stopped telling the story, and bowed his head. "I ask for your prayers. Pray for me. I do not want to be angry."

"No one can serve two masters…"

Matthew 6:24

What's your nationality? Around World Cup time, the question gets more pronounced. During the 2006, the Italians had good reason to cheer for their *Azzuri*. In this multi-ethnic city, however, they were not the only enthusiastic fans. We needed only to note the flags (or face paint colours) parading through the streets to know which teams were scheduled to meet that day. "Nationalism," according to sports writer Peter Berlin, "is the motor that drives the World Cup." (1)

In this age of globalization, national allegiances are not black and white. Match pairings make for interesting dilemmas, especially for immigrants. Our Serbian neighbour, for example, hung two flags out his window – one of his native land, and the other of his adopted country. A Ghanaian family in our church (who, I might add, gleefully needled us when their country's team beat the USA) with relatives in Dusseldorf, were torn when Italy met Germany. Prior to the Italy-United States match, our Italian friends wanted to know which side we would be supporting (I had to wait until the game started to sense which way my heart was leaning). After Italy's victory, the news showed fans whooping it up in far-off places like New York's Little Italy. Loyalty is no longer linked solely to geography.

Years ago, former British cabinet member Norman Tebbitt was incensed to see Pakistani, Indian or West Indian immigrants supporting the teams of their home countries when they played cricket against England. He devised what came to be known as 'The Tebbitt Test': that would-be Britons be asked what cricket team they supported, and if it was not England, they should not be given a passport.

It has been said that we Christians live as members of one culture, while being surrounded by another. "The church is a colony," Stanley Hauerwas and William H. Willimon write, "an island of one culture in the middle of another. In baptism our citizenship is transferred from one dominion to another, and we become, in whatever culture we find ourselves, resident aliens."(2) When our citizenship is transferred, what happens to our loyalties? Dilemmas of allegiance abound. At game time, which flag do we unfurl? Which team's success brings us out of our seat? Having lived in both dominions, in whose section of the stadium to do we sit? When the match begins, where does our heart lie?

"Save me, O God, for the waters have come up to my neck"

Psalm 65:1

Italy is home to the original 'rock and hard place'. Although not usually thought of as an Italian tale, Ulysses' journey in *The Odyssey* took him through the narrow strait between the boot of Italy and the island of Sicily.

According to legend, the two monsters that lurked below had, at one time, been creatures of great beauty. On the left side hid the monster Charybdis. A huge bladder of a creature, her face was all mouth and her arms and legs were flippers. Three times a day she swallowed the tide and spit it back out again. Sailors were terrified of getting caught as she spewed the sea out of her mouth, creating tremendous whirlpools in which no ship could survive.

On the right-hand side waited the monster Scylla. She was a huge, fleshy spider with twelve legs and six heads. With a wild hunger for human flesh, when any ship ventured near her, she would sweep the deck of sailors and devour them.

The Christian missionary Lesslie Newbigin compared the church to the ship of Ulysses. In an endless voyage between the rocks, the dangers await on both sides. One he called the *Scylla of isolationism*, the temptation for the church to remove itself from the world, to consider itself entirely different from the culture. The other side he called the *Charybdis of assimilation*, the lure of blending in completely with the surrounding culture.

Minority groups might also find that narrow strait an image for their own daily choices. Keeping distance from the dominant culture may maintain purity. But too much purity will mean isolation. Protect or blend? Criticize or acquiesce? First-generation immigrants find themselves closer to one side; their children farther into the current; their grandchildren almost to the other side.

In southern Italy debate has raged for decades about the feasibility of building a bridge over those troubled waters. For the time being, pilgrims and wayfarers will have to negotiate the narrow strait, keeping an eye to the currents and to the stars.

"Every knee shall bow…"

Philippians 2:10

Reflections on authority on Christ the King Monday

Italy's last dictator, Benito Mussolini, was executed and strung up by his feet in Milano's Piazza Loreto in April 1945. Not long after that, the Italians abolished the monarchy and set up a republic. The son of the last king of Italy is now something of a national embarrassment, often caught in one scandal or another. Since becoming a republic in 1948, the Italians have gone through some 60 governments, few of them lasting more than a year or two. Recently, after the longest run of any post-war government (five years), the voters had, apparently, had enough and voted in a new party. An onlooker might wonder if the Italians have something against authority.

The Milano-born historian Luigi Barzini once noted that Italians hold a "century-old ineradicable suspicion and mistrust of all governments, laws, regulations, and official authorities… In fact the individual Italian only obeys the rule that he has privately decided are just and useful."(3)

By all accounts, despite a populist reverence, few Italian Catholics heed the church's teachings on birth control. Members of the Protestant clergy strain to be anti-hierarchical – no collars, no titles, no bishops. While the African and Asian members of the church refer to us as *Pastor*, the Italian members call us David and Kristin. By church discipline, we elect a new church council every year. As one person told us, "We here in Italy don't want anyone to think too highly of themselves. So we find ways to remind one another not to act like royalty or the pope."

There aren't going to be too many coronations here. Then again, a rebellious spirit isn't exactly an Italian creation. People have been ignoring authority figures ever since Moses tried to guide a *stiff-necked* crowd through the wilderness. Seems like neck-bending or knee-bowing goes against some of our other inclinations.

Some claim – this king of kings.

*"Now you are the body of Christ
and individually members of it."*

I Corinthians 12:27

"While I was lying in that hospital bed last week, do you know what I missed most?" the elderly Italian Methodist woman asked. A few of us were sitting in her living room. On the walls around us were dozens of black and white photographs: deceased husband, sister, other relatives, large gatherings of people…

"What was it?" one of her friends asked.

"*La mia comunità*," she responded, "I missed my community most of all. You see, I *live* for my community." I was just trying to figure out exactly what she had meant. The Italian word *comunità* can mean the neighbourhood gang, a circle of friends, and in the case of the Protestants, the congregation.

As I tried to discern the context, someone else asked her about the photos on the wall.

As she began to explain each one, it was apparent that photos of family members were mixed in with other group shots. "That one was taken with the community in Palermo," she recounted, "and that other one is from the time we were a part of the community in Sondrio…." Ah, these were her former *congregations*.

Her father had been a Methodist pastor in each of those places. He had served throughout the turbulent fascist era, and had opposed fascism, even when the pressure mounted around him to sign a card of allegiance to Mussolini; something he had refused to do. Observers started appearing at the Sunday service, monitoring his sermons. They listened to the wording of his intercessory prayers. They took notes and menacingly surveyed the congregation.

"Because he never became a Fascist," she recounted, "we were at some risk as a family. I'll never forget hearing the president of the church council saying to my father one day, "You may not realize it, but you're being followed."

"How do you know that?" the pastor asked.

"Because we've been following you," the man replied.

"We? Who do you mean?"

"We, the members of the congregation. We follow every member of your family these days. We've been keeping an eye on each of you, wherever you go. We don't want anything to happen to you."

Now I understood a little better what she had meant by *comunità*.

"The Lord said to Moses, "Count all the firstborn Israelite males who are a month old or more and make a list of their names."

Numbers 3:40 (NIV)

After baptisms, I would be content merely to enter the necessary information on the church's computer data base. But the Church council and our colleague insist on the importance of entering the information in the *registro dei battesimi*. It's an old book, with fraying edges and warped by at least two floods. Inside, in varying handwriting of past ministers and council secretaries, in different shades and styles of calligraphy, names are entered and names are crossed out. There's also a *registro* that lists all worship services held in the church. Another one for *matrimoni*. Another for *funerali*. An overall *registro* listing church members. Each page is numbered. Each entry is numbered and dated. After a baptism or wedding, with a bit of a grumble, we pastors find the necessary book, muster our best handwriting, and join the generations of clergy who have laboured over these lists.

Only recently, we heard of one such Italian Methodist pastor who served a congregation in southern Italy during the Fascist period. As anti Semitism grew more vicious in Europe in the late 1930s, Jewish refugees began to flee across the Italian border. Yet what they found was an intensifying Italian brand of anti-Semitism which was becoming increasingly codified into Fascist laws. Methodist pastors tended to be anti-Fascist, which made them suspect by the Mussolini regime. That reputation sometimes caused Jewish refugees to seek the help of the Methodist churches.

Pastors and lay people were faced with daily choices; help a Jewish person in need and face arrest, or ignore the pleas all together. Church councils often began their regular orders of business with the question, "What shall we do with the Jews who are asking for our help?"

From time to time, this particular pastor was approached by Jewish families who asked for him to provide baptismal certificates for each of them. Proof of a 'conversion' would shield them from unjust harassment by the state. He would go to this shelf, and pull out the old baptismal *registro*, then enter the names one by one. Each convert was given an official register entry number. The pastor would fill out both halves of the certificate, carefully tear out one half along the perforation, give the person their ticket to safety, and put the book back on the shelf.

Over time, as the requests grew, in between the regular Methodist baptism entries, he began to leave several pages blank. If asked by the authorities to account for the gaps, he could confess careless bookkeeping. If, however, another person in need asked for a baptism certificate, he was prepared to issue it.

After hearing that story, opening those dusty old books has become a lot less tedious.

"...and he made him an elaborately embroidered coat."

Genesis 37:3 (*The Message*)

When we were first asked to serve in Milano, a friend wrote to us, "What will you be doing? Pastoral ministry to the fashion industry? Oh well, I suppose that even Giorgio Armani needs a chaplain once in a while."

I've never actually gotten close enough to Mr Armani to inquire about his spiritual needs. The closest we get to him or his cronies is seeing the occasional model in the grocery store (who is always buying yoghurt and alfalfa sprouts, or something of the like). There are also foreign students of fashion who come to study in Milano and find a home in the Methodist Church. Truth is, even though we live in 'the fashion capital of the world' (a moniker that some Parisians might protest), the closest we've come to any kind of runway is at the airport. Around the small circle of privileged villas and vias, city life here, like city life anywhere, buzzes on, oblivious. Sort of like living in the south Bronx and being asked, "What is it like to live in the financial capital of the world?"

But then again, we are parents of a teenager. And there are plenty of other foreign teenagers in this congregation. As well as any Italian kid, they learn fast what's in and what's not. (Current fads: *Dolce and Gabbana* belt, *Diesel* jeans, and sneakers by *Nike* or *Converse*.) Immigrant parents who wince to see their children kept to the fringes find brand names an alluring point of entry. Yet, most of the families we know can only afford the Chinese knock-offs. So, whether it's purchased in the upscale shops in the city's Galleria, or from under a canvas stall at the Saturday afternoon market, if it's got the right letters, that's all that matters. The devil may not actually wear *Prada*, but certainly creates a lot of peer pressure to do so.

The desire to fit the fashion mould so tightly surprises some in the industry. Why, in a city packed with creative alternative design labels, do young people choose from such a narrow cross section of brands? Some say that the Italian emphasis on the *bella figura* (good impression) is so strong that the fear of being ridiculed outweighs any freedom of selection. Among teenagers especially, the aversion to being singled out drives many to the flock of conformity. A sadder commentary still comes from an interview with a young designer: "Wearing expensive jeans gives you a sense of belonging. Wearing labels provides a sense of belonging to a group. It's a way of identifying yourself..." (4)

Finding an identity. Feeling alone. Fitting in. Being accepted. Seeking a place to belong. Giorgio and Company may have created a need for a kind of chaplaincy after all. This, however, is nothing new. Ever since Jacob gave Joseph that coat, eate clothes have been causing problems.

*"O God, the nations have come into your inheritance;
they have defiled your holy temple…"*

Psalm 79:1

"Can you tell me about this church?" I held up a recent issue of News-
week magazine and pointed to the photo on page 53. The man did not
hesitate. "Oh yes, *La Chiesa Sconsacrata* – I know it well. It's on Via Piero
Della Francesca. He led me to an intersection, then pointed: "There, see
it?"

I thanked him, walked across the street, and looked up. The church was
crammed in between two more modern buildings. Its brick façade was
divided by several shafts of marble which soared up to a circular stained
glass window. Above the peak of the roof, a slender bell tower pointed to
the sky. It was exactly 3:00pm, but no sound came from the clock on the
tower.

The large wooden doors were open, and I stepped into the foyer. On the
wall above a white upholstered couch was a stone plaque with an inscrip-
tion in Latin:

SANCTVARIVM HOC
D JOSEPHO A PACE
DICATUM
REMOTO INTERINALI SACELLO
DIE 2 OCTOBRIS 1927

Inside, ornate floor tiles with Celtic designs lined the centre aisle. I
walked slowly to the front, noticing the immense chandelier hanging
overhead. Up the three steps to the chancel area where…the man behind
the large wooden bar shook a tumbler. The bottles behind him were
neatly arranged on glass-tiered shelves, each with different coloured
lights, giving the display a rainbow effect. In the centre, above the highest
shelf was a large mirror, draped on either side by satin curtains. On the
mirror were the words 'Don Q Puerto Rican Rum' embossed in gold
lettering. Higher still, a silver disco ball rotated. Near the ceiling on either
side of the former altar were stage lights aimed at the dance floor. On the
capitals of the column, beneath several coats of gold enamel, the Christian symbol 'IHS' was still barely visible. At either end of the bar, where
at one time incense might have wafted up during worship, sat two artifi-
cial smoke machines. The bartender looked up: "What will you have?" He
motioned to Harp, Guinness and Nastro Azzurro on tap. "Uh, nothing,
thanks."

Some thirty circular tables, each surrounded by plush high-backed chairs were positioned throughout the hall. In the former side chapels where presumably, the confessional booths had once been, were semi-circular tables for more private *tête á têtes*. Along the balcony were 50 or so bar stools. Behind them were more tables and chairs, and behind them, brightly-lit signs for the men and women's toilettes.

It was getting close to the time for my meeting, so I left. Outside the door, I read the sign: 'Il Gattopardo Café – Happy Hour from 18:00 – 22:00 – Disco Bar from 22:00 – 05:00'. Below hung one other sign: *Si Prega La Gentile Clientela di Evitare Schiamazzi Notturni Davanti Al Locale* (We ask our kind clientele to avoid night-time racket on the premises).

I nodded to the bartender and exited. Outside, an old man dressed in a tie was shuffling by. He paused, made the sign of the cross, and continued. "Excuse me, sir," I said, "What do you know about this church?"

"Ah, it was where I used to come to mass", he replied. "But then – it must have been 15 years ago now – they changed it to this. A different kind of people come here now."

> *"Pilate asked them, "Shall I crucify your King?"*
> *The chief priests answered, "We have no king but the emperor".*

John 19:15

Even though Milano is a good day's journey north from Rome, the Eternal City is a very present reality here up north. Everyone has a brother or a cousin who lives in Rome. Tourists come through Milano on their way to Rome. Some of Milano's biggest soccer rivals are teams from Rome. News about parliament or Alitalia often emanates from Rome. So often do we hear about goings-on in Rome that on occasion, a mention of 'The Letter to the Romans' makes us wonder at first: which Romans? Oh, *those* Romans.

Which was what made this year's reading of the crucifixion story so strange. Maybe the frequency with which we hear reference to modern-day Rome made us notice how prominent a role Rome or the Romans play in the narrative of Christ's passion. When Judas came to the garden, it was a group of Roman police, soldiers and church leaders. Caiaphas, the chief priest, had been put in place by the Roman governor. Jesus stood before Caesar's man on the ground in Jerusalem to be interrogated. In the end, Roman soldiers whipped him, forced him to carry the cross, nailed his hands to the wood, mocked him and played with his clothes while he was dying. In an angry cast of thousands, the Romans of the passion narrative are front and centre. They represent an empire, both religious and heathen, arrogant and naïve, both fearful and ruthless in their response to a Palestinian trouble-maker. Despite the human frailty of its leaders, it had the power to dispatch all its final verdicts with steely precision. And in recounting the tale in Good Friday worship, each references to Rome or its citizens seemed to draw an unsettling link between us and the least likeable characters in the story.

Here, in the ancient Roman outpost of Mediolanum (now Milano) where Roman gates still stand, people continue to view Rome as the centre of things. On the lips of immigrants, "Rome" holds the administrative power: "I'm waiting to see if the office in Rome will issue my permission to stay" Church leaders (and not just Catholic ones) still look to Rome for guidance: "We can't do that without approval from the Methodist office in Rome…or… all that liturgy is issued from Rome…" Rome is the seat of a lumbering bureaucracy and the cozy relationship between church and state. News is broadcast from Rome, business deals are made in Rome, and train travel from north to south travels through Rome's *Termini*. Perhaps not *all*, but many roads still lead to and from Rome.

Which, it would seem, is the tacit complaint against empires. Whether we wish it or not, our lives depend upon the empire. It touches all aspects of life. Its economic reach, its cultural influence, its political clout, and yes, its military might extends to distant shores. A civilization so vast is bound to kindle a boisterous ambivalence. We depend on the empire, even delight in its privileges, but are wary that it has too tight a grip on all beneath its flag.

Someone has suggested that we like to listen to the Christmas story because we project ourselves on to the more congenial, docile figures in the story: an innocent baby, a adoring mother, a concerned father; when, in fact, we may have more in common with the empire which surrounded them. And on this Good Friday, just as I may have been trying to find myself huddled around a fire in Caiaphas' courtyard, warming my hands alongside Simon Peter, someone approaches and asks, "Say, aren't you one of them?" And as I stammer a reply, my inquisitor follows up, "No, I mean, aren't you one of those Romans?"

After each reading from John that night, a candle was snuffed. To the light of the last lone flame, we heard one final reference to the Romans: a recruit for the occupation forces who looked up at the dying man on the cross and realized, *Surely this was the Son of God.* Such are the contradictions of those of us in the empire.

Together, When Our Religious Labels Differ

"...it was called Babel,
because there the Lord confused the language..."

Genesis 11:9

January...

The Methodist Church hosts ecumenical worship for the Week of Christian Unity. Needing some additional microphones to add to their own two, the Methodists ask the neighbouring Catholic parish for help. The Catholics lend two hand-held microphones to the Methodists for the occasion.

February...

The Methodists notice that one of their hand-held microphones is not working. They change the batteries, but to no avail. They send the microphone out to a technician. He finds no problem but comes to the church to inspect the sound system. The mysterious problem remains unresolved.

Meanwhile...

The Catholics notice that one of *their* hand-held microphones is not working. They change the batteries, but to no avail. They send the microphone out to a technician. He finds no problem but comes to the church to inspect the sound system. The mysterious problem remains unresolved.

Some time in March...

The Methodist pastor bumps into the Catholic priest in Piazza Minitti. They exchange pleasantries and talk about their respective church activities. "We're getting ready for our Lenten services and we were testing our microphones. One of them doesn't work. Might we borrow yours – one of those hand-held ones?"

"Yeah, sure. Oh wait, our hand-held mike is giving us problems, too."

"Oh, that's too bad. I guess we'll have to... Wait a minute." Both holy men receive an epiphany at the same moment. A blinding light of realization appears over each of their heads. "Be right back."

Moments later, they return to Piazza Minniti. As if in some audio-electric inter-faith duel, both are brandishing identical black microphones.

"This wouldn't, by any chance, be *yours*, would it?"

"And this deceptively similar-looking one couldn't possibly be *yours*, could it?"

"That must be why *our* members have noticed our homilies lately have included a lot of quotes from Martin Luther."

"And that would explain why, at the end of our Methodist worship service lately, we've been hearing somebody singing the *Ave Maria*."

*"Clap your hands, all you peoples;
shout to God with loud songs of joy"*

Psalm 47:1

"And your choir," the elderly Signore Rossi said, as he led us briskly down the sidewalk, "will sing...over here." He was the neighbourhood organizer of the 'White Night', an all-night shopping and entertainment festival marking the summer solstice. He had asked the international choir from the Methodist Church to sing that night, and we were given the 10:15pm place on the docket 'at a place to be designated'. Church members had changed worked schedules to come. Hannah and Aidan got to stay up late to sing with the group. Our 'designated place' turned out to be curbside, facing the... (did Signore Rossi have a twinkle in his eye?)... *Macelleria Islamica* (Islamic butcher shop). There, on a plaque above the door, written in Arabic, the words 'There is no divinity but Allah, and Muhammad is his Prophet'.

We unpacked our guitars, got out our music and shuffled into place. Ten or so middle-eastern men glanced up at our group. Others came out of the butcher shop to see who we were. After our introduction as "the Methodists from down the street who will sing Christian songs," we broke into our multi-lingual, albeit Christocentric, repertoire: "Give Me Oil in My Lamp... Nurtured by the Spirit... The Message We Proclaim... In His Name We Have a Victory... Lord, I Lift Your Name on High..." The men started clapping in time to the rhythm. The butcher lifted his small son up onto the counter to see, and rocked him gently back and forth in time with the music.

After several songs, our audience (which had grown) shouted *"bis!"* ("encore!"). We sang some more, grinning at the irony of our placement. In a neighbourhood filled with angry graffiti; not far from a Muslim mosque whose community is outraged about a CIA abduction of its Imam last year; during a summer when events in London and Egypt, and threats in Italy have everyone on edge, Signore Rossi had plotted less a clash of civilizations, and more an encounter of unknown neighbours across the back fence. We trust God to use it as an introduction.

"…the Lord is in his holy temple;
let all the earth keep silence before him!"

Habakkuk 2:20

This city of 1.3 million people creates a Babel of tongues and language. From the not-so-sound-proof booths of the international phone centres, people converse with far-away relatives in Mandarin and Portuguese. The advertisers, fully aware that their targets are no longer Italian-speakers, fill billboard and airwaves with messages in Arabic and Sinhalese. Even in church, praying the Lord's prayer in our 15 or so various languages can either sound like a chorus or a cacophony.

Every September a group of Franciscan brothers sets up a tent outside the Duomo. They invite all religious groups in the city, distribute pamphlets, and hang posters. "There are too many words in circulation," their invitations read, "…Many of them make dialogue difficult and intolerance grows between people who are different than we…" They invite into the tent, believers and unbelievers, observers of various faiths, members of different political parties; not to pray or make speeches ("which can so easily offend another's sensibilities"), but to be silent together.

On this particular day, German and Italian youth stood at the entrance of the tent and handed out pages of selected readings. A young woman stretched out her hand towards a guest book, inviting persons to add their own words about peace. Inside, Jewish rabbis nodded with smiles to Catholic brothers from Assisi. A young novitiate shared rug space with a middle-aged Muslim man. School children scooted over to make room for people with walkers. Some people sat with their eyes closed while others quietly read selections by everyone from Gandhi to Bonhoeffer, from the Catholic Archbishop to the Milano Waldensian community. But for some gentle music and the occasional *vespa* buzzing across the piazza, all was silent.

"Silence can become the universal language, the communal space, the prelude to encounter, to listening and to discussion," we were reminded. "All encounters that are real and sincere begin in silence."

And for those few minutes, under that canvas, Milano seemed a little more harmonious.

"…if you sin against God, who is around to help?"

I Samuel 2:25 (The Message)

"But, *tesoro* (treasure), there are times when I need a priest," she said. Her hand, wearing an engagement ring, touched his.

"It is not necessary to have a priest," he answered. "As a Protestant, I don't believe that I have to go through a priest to talk to God."

"But how do you confess your sins?"

"I can do it in church. We pray the prayer of confession every Sunday."

"But can you really do that yourself, I mean *really* confess?"

Ah, the role of the clergy. In Italy, any 'inter-faith' discussion (as Catholic-Protestant dialogue is called here) ends up here. Priests, wearing their clerical collars, sit across from their Protestant pastoral colleagues, sporting ties or open-neck shirts. Catholic parish meetings are usually conducted by the priest. In Protestant congregations meetings are run by the lay president of the church council. While a Catholic woman preparing for the Women's World Day of Prayer says, "I'll have to ask my priest," her Protestant counterpart responds, "I'll talk it over with the other women in my group." In an obvious swipe at the Pope, one Waldensian brochure reads, "The Church's task is to serve, not to represent God, who needs neither representatives nor a Vicar of Christ."

"You're an intelligent woman," the young man implored his fiancée. "You do not need to go to your priest for everything. I mean, you own a Bible. You can read it yourself. You don't have to wait for the Father to do those things for you…"

"Yes, I know," she responded. "But how do I put this?" She paused. "I don't always think about God. I don't even read the Bible very often. It's like, if I were left on my own, I would fall into bad habits. I need someone who reminds me about the important things. I need someone who reminds me about God.

"… You and your household"

Acts 16:31

On this Week of Prayer for Christian Unity,
the gracious invitation goes out to the city's faithful
from Father Dmitri: come join us for vespers.

We, cut from the cloths of Rome and Reformation,
can feel a bit un-Orthodox in this hallowed hall;
sounding out the Cyrillic text, peering at the icons.

Easy to feel more like a visitor than a participant –
like an upper-deck spectator holding binoculars,
trying to make sense of the action below.

Ecumenism… from the Greek *oikos*…house;
we're in the house, but in distant rooms, perhaps.
Prayers abound, but unity?

I am seated in the corner, behind the choir,
three women – heads covered – are singing the liturgy;
one shines a penlight on the dog-eared music pages.

Their voices rise and fall together in fifths,
a nod of the head, an occasional shared glance,
and their melodies dance in nimble steps.

With his back to us, we strain to overhear the priest's chants:
Gospodi pomilui, Gospodi pomilui, Gospodi pomilui.
Mind wanders. Legs ache. Thoughts drift to home.

Harmony cracks, two voices trail off;
quick shoulder shrug, grimace, embarrassed silence;
then, a spurted laugh, solemnity uncorked.

Priest's mike goes out; assistant wrestles with a replacement;
taps it, no sound, scampers to the back.
Suddenly, the house is feeling more like home.

More disarray within the shawled choir.
One gives another a staccato glare, a silent dart -
a mode of communication used in many a church.

The view from this corner is not so removed after all.
From here, Father Dmitri's mismatched socks are visible,
and there's a clear view into the back room of the *oikos*.

"You shall keep my Sabbaths and reverence my sanctuary…"

Leviticus 26:2

The august group of ecumenical dignitaries processed up the long, centre aisle of Milano's Duomo cathedral. On this first day of January, the Cardinal had invited representatives from the Orthodox and Protestant communities to join the bishops, priests, and throngs of Catholic faithful for the annual New Year's Day mass. Viewed from above, the assembly would include several round black hats, a slew of triangular white hats, various albs and vestments, one prominent red skull cap, and inexplicably… two smaller heads, with no hats.

The latter's liturgical garb seemed more in keeping with an elementary and middle school classroom. They attracted considerable attention on the solemn approach to the altar. As they made their way past the eighth or ninth pillar of the cathedral, some people in the pews whispered, *"Chi sono?"* ("Who are they?"). The question may have been directed at the two children, or at their two confused parents who held their hands. *The invitation did say ecumenical pastors AND their families, didn't it? Were we not supposed to sit all together? Wouldn't one of the organizers in the sacristy have said anything? Perhaps they didn't notice?* So far, despite their feeling a bit under-dressed and over-Reformed, there had been no accusations of heresy or queue-jumping.

One of the Cardinal's six or seven attendants motioned to the ecumenical parade to ascend the altar steps. After various shows of reverence – the Catholic sign of the cross, the inverse Orthodox motion, slight bows of the head, and two nervous glances up at parental guides – the VIPs were directed past the porcelain figure of the Christ child in the manger, to several semi-circular pews facing the congregation. The Cardinal sat in the throne to the group's left. The steel-faced priest who acted as Liturgical Choreographer nodded, and in perfect synchrony all the attendants lowered themselves into the pew in front of the ecumenical guests.

With a flourish of incense and chanting, the mass got underway. From their perch in the front, the guests could see the thousands of congregants, in this, the second largest Catholic cathedral in the world in the second largest diocese in the world. The Cardinal delivered his greetings to the delegation, took a sip of water from the cup handed to him on a silver tray by one of the attendants, and launched into his New Year's address. Somewhere between the seventh and eighth pages, the Eritrean Orthodox priest began to play with his prayer beads. The Romanian Orthodox priest readjusted the tunic around his shoulders, the Salvation Army Captain pulled at his tight collar. A slightly shorter guest titled the drawing on his sketch pad: 'The pope's staff', while another young Methodist representative next to him doodled a fairy picnic.

"And in the New Year, may we, the faithful of God, recommit ourselves to..." The incense acolytes shuffled their feet. The Ethiopian priest let out a little sigh. From somewhere in the Protestant section, someone whispered, "I spy with my little eye... the face of a lion in the wall..." The Mass Monitor, seated facing the congregation, with his back to the ecumenical guests, wheeled around and glared. He repeated his surveillance, almost as if to check that no one was making off with a silver candelabra. Every so often, he would glance at his watch, then catch the eye of his regimen of attendants, then point to a spot in the floor where presumably the next segment of pageantry would begin.

After finishing his address, the Cardinal, assisted by a priest who picked up the edges of his flowing white robes, made his way over to the altar. In a fresh cloud of incense, he recited the words of institution: "On the night when he was betrayed, Jesus took bread, broke it..." Bells, more incense. More clipped instructions from the Traffic Cop. His clerical squad fanned out around the altar, prepared for the hand-off.

With the host raised in his hands, the thousands of worshippers hushed. There was no usual sound of rustling or shifting of weight, no coughing or sneezing. A holy silence, and then... a hiccup; loud, startling, and very youthful. The little hiccup seemed to find every sacred corner of the cathedral in which to reverberate. The Monitor jerked his head around in the direction of the guests. Four Protestant members of the delegation slunk down a bit in the pew. One of them, in a hapless (and very un-ecumenical) effort to deflect the accusation, gave a prosecutorial look at one of the Romanian priests.

The Inspector slowly lifted his eyes from the nervous line-up. As he was turning back towards the altar, his eyes seemed to rest briefly on the baby Jesus, then on the back of the Cardinal's robes... Then, with a squint of a detective, quickly back to the porcelain child in the manger. He cocked his head and looked back at the suspects. And for an instant, it was hard to tell if a slight smile flickered across his face.

"Other seeds fell on good soil and brought forth grain..."

Matthew 13:8

"And this evening, we welcome to the Methodist Church the choir from the Parrocchia di Sant' Ildefonso. It is their first time to participate in an event during the Week of Prayer for Christian Unity."

Rewind the clock nearly ten years. Churches all over the city of Milano prepare to host some 50,000 young people at the winter Taizè 'Pilgrimage of Trust'. An active Methodist laywoman named Anne decides she would like to host several youths in her apartment for the week. She goes to the Catholic church in her neighbourhood, Sant' Ildefonso, and signs up.

The Taizè prayer gatherings take place across the city. Anne accompanies her young Polish guests to the Church of Sant' Ildefonso one evening and finds out that they are short of musicians. The next evening she brings her flute and accompanies the chants. In the process she gradually gets to know some of the members of the parish.

Years later, the choir at Sant' Ildefonso is looking to expand their repertoire. Their director remembers a Protestant woman who had once played her flute in their parish. He tracks her down and asks her to come to a choir practice. She teaches them some Protestant anthems.

A year of working together goes by. Anne is asked to co-direct the choir. She works with the group in learning songs from the Russian Orthodox, American Gospel and African praise traditions. They sing for mass and occasional other events within their parish.

Anne finds out about the forthcoming ecumenical choir concert during the Week of Prayer for Christian Unity. This year it is being held at her own Chiesa Evangelica Metodista. She suggests to the Sant' Ildefonso choir that they might think about joining in. They respond enthusiastically, and prepare two pieces for the event.

That night, after the worship service finishes, choir members sip coffee with people from various churches – Romanian Orthodox, Korean Baptist, Catholic, Methodist, Russian Orthodox – they have never met.

A seed falls, apparently without consequence. It is presumed to have landed on a rock, blown away or carried off by birds. By some miracle, though, it takes root, sprouts, grows, and bears fruit of its own.

"So they took branches of palm trees and went out to meet him,
shouting, "Hosanna! Blessed is the one who comes
in the name of the Lord – the King of Israel!"

John 12:13

It wasn't easy to get palms for Palm Sunday our first year here. In our previous church lives, we'd been rather spoiled. Somewhere during Epiphany we might get a reminder from a Christian supply store, asking us if we wanted to keep the palm order the same as last year's. A fax or a call from a church secretary, and boxes of palm branches would appear sometime towards the end of Lent, ready to use.

So, when no such box magically appeared at the Methodist Church of Milano, we asked one of the Italian members when we might expect them to arrive. "Oh, that's a Catholic thing, palms," he said. "We Protestants don't use them here in Italy." While we respected the customs of our Italian brothers and sisters, we also knew that for the large majority of Africans, Asians and North and South Americans in the congregation, there would be an expectation of palms. So we set out in search of some palms. How hard could it be, anyway? There are palm trees all over Italy.

First stop, a florist: *I've got this potted palm plant. It needs direct sun light.* (But nothing in bulk.) Perhaps a garden store? *This palm tree goes nice in a foyer.* (But not to be cut up in little bits and distributed.) How about the parish priest? *Oh, I wished you'd told me sooner. I've only got enough for our parish. But why don't you try the Duomo?*

By this time it was Saturday, and Milano's *Duomo* (Cathedral) seemed like our only option. I took the subway downtown and found my way to the sacristy, stumbled my way through an introduction to the robed man behind the desk and asked if they might have any extra palms for tomorrow. His eyes squinted. "Palms? No. Only the archbishop carries a palm branch. What do you want them for?" I tried to rephrase my explanation. "What we've got," the attendant said, "is bundles of olive branches. But we need them for the thousands of people that will come to mass tomorrow." He decided to make a few phone calls. Several minutes later he hung up the phone: "The cardinal says OK. The problem is that they're not yet blessed for tomorrow." I assured him that that would not be a problem. "*Va bene*, go pick out yourself a bundle. Just don't give any out this afternoon. You know, their not being blessed and all…" I thanked him profusely, left a gift in the offering plate, and carried them rather self-consciously onto the subway. The next morning our Methodist procession to *Hosanna, Loud Hosanna* had an ecumenical touch.

The following day the parish priest phoned: "Just wondered if you got any palms?" I explained that we had. "Well, I'm going to put an early order in for next year's palms, bigger than this year's. That way, you can have some, and you won't have to go begging to the Cardinal!"

On the wall of one of the catacombed tunnels beneath Rome, there is a fresco of a palm branch. Apparently, for the early Christians, the symbol was not only a reminder of the procession into Jerusalem. It was a symbol of victory.

*"Out beyond ideas of right doing and wrong doing there is a field.
I'll meet you there."*

Rumi (1)

Interfaith gathering
draws the regulars:
seasoned delegates
and perpetual ecumenics.
Off their prayer mats,
out of their cathedrals,
away from their *minyans,*
detached from their consistories,
they take their usual seats.

Quiet, please!
Let us come to order.
Last meeting's minutes
are read;
then reports and resolutions,
dates and declarations,
all adjusted for grammar,
checked for theological concordance,
and governed by protocol.

Per favore! Quiet! Order!
Voices outside,
interfaith stragglers
beneath the window,
disturb the meeting:
an imam,
a rabbi.
a priest –
laughing…
at something.

Together, in Conflict

"Real community is painful."

Jean Vanier (1)

"Bastardo," he whispered it under his breath, his one fist clenched. It was not the kind of comment usually heard at a church meeting like this. While his seething description of the person seated across the table will probably not appear in the minutes, perhaps it should. It captured the tone of this particular discussion.

So much behind his anger. For him, this was no casual, esoteric conversation about any particular ethical issue. Rather, it was about something that is central to his own identity.

"Bastardo," again. His thrust the ballpoint pen into its cap, as if a sign that he was through. "No more participation. No more. I've had it. I had expected more of you, but apparently, I was wrong."

Expectations are dangerous in this Christian community-thing. We can project onto the other who we *think* they are. We can interpret shared smiles and laughter as signs that we really are, when it all comes down to it, the same people. We can almost imagine that a friendship has blossomed between us before we do the hard work to forge one.

Conversations like tonight's feel more like a rupture. Illusions are shattered: *I never knew you believed that so strongly! I had no idea you held that opinion. You are not who I thought you were. I mistook our friendly banter as agreement.* The anger can burn away the false fellowship and reveal what is really there: *I suppose I knew all along how different we were. Now I see it clearly, very clearly. Maybe you were hoping to change me. Don't count on it. I guess I won't change you either…*

Bastardo.

Now what? Maybe the *real* stuff, the *real* community, starts from here.

"Can we be different but not alienated?
Only if there is mutuality in our relating."

Katie G. Cannon (2)

Integration, says the host, is when you finally feel at home with us. It is when you have learned to speak our language (after all, your children already speak our language so well… they like our foods… they are more Italian than we are!). We'll even help you to integrate: we will help you learn our language. You'll need it in order to function here.

Thank you, says the guest. Your hospitality is very kind. It is very hard to make it here. But it is nice to know that you are so willing to help us. Say, would it be OK if we brought a few of our practices into the church?

Certainly! Well, exactly what kind of practices are you talking about? I mean, we have already accepted a few changes into our church because of you foreigners: we pass the peace now; we have a little longer worship service. We'll even clap once in a while. But how many changes do you expect us to make? It is, after all, our church. It's the church of our parents, our grandparents.

No offence, but when we have our worship together, we feel a little, well, stifled. We like to sing and praise. We normally don't use bulletins in order to worship. We would prefer to dance when we receive the offering.

We have accommodated you – like when we worship together, we even allow for it to be in two languages. That means we have to sit through long sermons in English that we don't even understand. One day, you will not need that, because you will be so well-integrated. We will all be speaking Italian.

We *are* wanting to learn Italian. But we will never be Italian. We will always want to have opportunities to worship in our own language. We just don't feel like we worship God when we do it in your style.

But that is separation. The Body is to be one. We should be together!

Yes, but does being one body mean we are *always* together? Can there be times when we worship the way we want to worship?

Are you ungrateful? Why don't you want to integrate?

We *do* want to integrate!

What do you mean exactly by integration?

How about you – what do *you* mean?

*"And the Lord said to Rebekah, "Two nations are in your womb,
and two peoples born of you shall be divided;
the one shall be stronger than the other…"*

Genesis 25:23

On the surface, Jacob and Esau could have made a go of it. They each had their roles. They each had their responsibilities. Their family – their community – seemed to be chugging along well enough. But the friction between them may have been inevitable, foreshadowed in the darkness of their mother's womb where they had 'struggled together within her'. A little competition, a little deceit, one of them getting Dad's special blessing, and the envy was enough to threaten any relationship between them.

Envy creeps into *our* communal life, too. Oh, we use high fallutin' terms like *reciprocity, balanced representation, responsibility-sharing, interculturality, mutuality* to feign being above all-out brotherly wrestling matches like Jacob and Esau's. In a congregation as diverse as ours, it is a rare thing when one person's accomplishment can elicit universal celebration. Or when one cultural component seems to be gaining members or recognition or clout the other cultural components take notice. Just under the surface, I wonder if your day in the sun translates into my day in the shadows. Your gains, your moment of joy, your day of satisfaction will not necessarily coincide with my gains, my moment of joy or my day of satisfaction. In fact, they may lag years behind one another. And that's not easy.

Before we got married, a pastor cautioned us to beware of competition. Competition? With an enamoured look into one another's eyes, we scoffed at the thought. That's all well and good, said the wise pastor, but what about those Sundays after church, when the two of you stand together at the sanctuary door, and some parishioner says to one of you, "What a sermon you just preached! It was amazing! Incredible! The best I've ever heard!" Will you both hear those words in the same way? Loving a spouse, or for that matter thy neighbour as thyself, can be easily derailed by envy.

Oh, the power of a truly affirming word! The impact of an authentic compliment! The immeasurable riches of an ego checked! The liberating freedom of admitting that she really is better at certain things than I am… The community-building result of someone saying, "This is not all about me. This is about the church". Something like that might have shocked the feuding brothers just enough to loosen his half-Nelson on the other.

*"Or look at ships: though they are so large that it takes
strong winds to drive them,
yet they are guided by a very small rudder
wherever the will of the pilot directs.
So also the tongue is a small member,
yet it boasts of great exploits."*

James 3:4-5

If one of the ancient symbols of the church is a ship, our congregation would probably be closer to an outrigger canoe. Steamships are more resilient. Tugboats more durable. Canoes, on the other hand, rock with the slightest wave. If someone goes wobbly on the starboard side, someone else on the port side is liable to fall in.

All the paddlers seem to speak a different language. They may be paddling next to one another, but they really don't know one another too well yet. There's a real desire to paddle together, but with all those different paddling styles and orders being barked in various languages, it doesn't take much to upset the balance.

With an equilibrium so fragile, one quick turn of the rudder can send us all tumbling. Take, for example, a few choice phrases used by some crew members lately: *Her kind are always unreliable... those bowls that went missing in the kitchen; you know what probably happened to them. It was that group of ... that was in here last week.... you know them, they are all rude.* Even more innocuous interchanges can hold, at their deepest layers, perceived insults: *Would you tell your friends that the plastic has to be separated from the glass? (MY friends? What makes her think that it was MY friends that mixed up the recycling?)* Ouch.

Unbridled tongues (one of James' favourite phrases) can destroy the trust that is the foundation of any cross-cultural friendship. *If that's what you really think of us, then what am I to make of all your past pleasantness? Was it all just a polite charade? Do you really not want me (and my 'kind') around?*

Full disclosure has its value, and probably its time and place. But honesty (at the wrong time or place) can be overrated. A little careful bridling can keep the ship on even-keel. Otherwise, a sudden shift of the rudder may have us all in the drink.

"Jesus said to Peter, "Put your sword back into its sheath"

John 18:11

"There is much publicity about the importance to the peace process of the disarmament of guns, but just as difficult to achieve and just as crucial is the disarmament of minds."

Susan McEwan (3)

The two congregation members had finally seemed to have moved past their feud. They had clashed over a small issue, which, agitated by differences of culture, tradition and temperament, erupted into a full-scale battle. It was clear to each that the other was entirely wrong, motivated by power, and totally insensitive to the needs of 'my people'.

The open warfare de-escalated into an icy stand-off. When possible they avoided one another, but kept up their war of words to anyone who would listen. Often the narrative was the same, with the emphases on the same offences. Time, more than any noticeable effort to forgive or reconcile, ratcheted down their tension. Over several years, the issues and anger seemed to fade. In meeting settings, where others were present, the two even talked to one another. By no means fast friends, they had at least reached a working relationship. The swords had been put back into their sheaths.

But sheathed swords are still swords. Recently, a disagreement occurred involving one of the original feuding parties. The other was present, and as if unable to fight the addiction to nostalgic malicious pleasure, began to join in the criticism going on in the room. Then, suddenly embarrassed, she sighed, hung her head, and said to no one in particular: "I'm sorry. I couldn't help myself." Some kind of inner penitence began, but the damage was done.

The mind is a difficult thing to disarm. While one lobe may be open to forgive, the memory lobe remains locked. As if by reflex, we can so easily reach for the familiar contour of the sword handle. Perhaps the best we can do is to ask God for the will power to keep the sword in its sheath.

*"When the hour came, he took his place at the table,
and the apostles with him."*

Luke 22:14

Sunday school teachers, parents, pastors, lay people, men, women, Africans, Italians, Americans, Filipinos – if our *cultural* diversity was not already obvious enough, discussing whether or not children should receive the Lord's Supper reminded us of how differently we approach the faith.

Children do not yet understand what Holy Communion means, said some.

Neither do we adults fully grasp it either, said others.

They will appreciate it more if they have to wait for it.

But they will feel excluded when they see the rest of us receiving it.

They don't see the specialness of it; they think it's a snack.

They will learn reverence by observing reverence in us.

Some quoted Paul: *"Whoever, therefore,"* the apostle wrote to the Corinthians, *"eats the bread and drinks the cup of the Lord in an unworthy manner will be answerable for the body and blood of the Lord."*

Yes, but he is speaking about unrighteous behaviour in adults.

No, he means that anyone who received the elements in an unappreciative manner would be cursed.

Others cited Matthew's Gospel: *"Then the little children were brought to him in order that he might lay his hands on them and pray."*

Yes, but that was for a blessing, not for the Holy Supper.

But when the disciples held them back, Jesus instructed the disciples to let the children through.

One man stood up dramatically, walked over to a poster which showed Jesus at the last supper. He said, "Who do we see there with the Lord? We see the disciples. Only the disciples! There were no children!"

A sister muttered, "Yes, but we don't see women there either. And eventually the church thought it was all right for women to receive communion."

How much are discussions like these battles between our grandparents, or our seminaries, or our most beloved former pastors? How much is a clash of how we choose to interpret Scripture, and how much is it a lack of having chosen anything, rather accepting that which has been passed on to us as absolute truth? Do we parry with scripture, or rather with the culture that taught it to us? What do we do when Jesus did not issue a clear beatitude on our behalf?

What would have happened at that first/last supper, had a little hand knocked on the door during the first course: *Dad, are you guys almost finished?* Or what if the young child of one of the servants in the house happened to sidle up to the table? Would she have been asked to wait outside? How would Jesus have reacted to her presence? And when the bread and the wine were passed around, would those who had agreed with the Master's decision been able to partake alongside those who did not?

(to be continued...)

"If your heart is as my heart then give me your hand"

John Wesley, sermon, 'A Catholic Spirit'

After months of discussion about children and Holy Communion, and in the autonomy that the Italian reformed tradition grants to individual congregations, we reached a compromise: the congregation would prefer that only confirmed children should commune, but if parents had strong feelings about their children receiving, no one would be denied. No one seemed truly satisfied. One result of the cumbersome agreement was the necessity of conversations with individual families, involving teaching and sensitivity to their traditions. Another result was that people of opposing views would have to commune together.

The Lord's Supper became a bit awkward. We three pastors took to alternating in the role of distributing the bread, sharing the role as point person for any children who might come forward. A quick word with the parent or accompanying adult; then instantaneous discernment for hand on the head or a handful of bread. For persons in both theological camps, the Eucharist became some kind of spectator sport – would he or wouldn't he? Should she or shouldn't she? Sadly, the sacrament was becoming more calculation than celebration.

Somewhere during that period, a theology professor from Ghana visited. He was asked his advice for congregations who are made up of people who do not all interpret the Bible in the same manner. He acknowledged that this is a reality in many congregations, but that it need not be a cause for division, rather for a new kind of unity. "It is vital for people to stay in dialogue with one another about their different opinions," he said, "not to distance themselves from someone with whom they do not agree. When we enter into dialogue, we let go of some things, leave some things behind. Neither side wins or loses, but both change. When two chemicals come together," Professor Asante concluded, "neither one remains the same; they react with one another and form a new compound." The Holy Spirit is at work, creating something new.

A month or so later, a few minutes before worship was to begin, we got word that the designated communion steward could not come to church. Hastily, I asked one of the men in the congregation to step in. When it was time to distribute the elements, I took the bread and handed him the chalice. Only as parents with children began to come forward did it dawn on me that, months earlier, he had made his opinion clear, that children should *not* receive communion.

I deliberated my way the distribution of bread. Suddenly I was aware of his tall African frame stooped down. His arms were extended, his big hands offering the chalice to a three-year-old girl. She looked at his face, then dipped her bread in the cup. Then she grinned. It could very well have been in response to the big grin on his face.

Something new.

*"So when you are offering your gift at the altar, if you remember
that your brother or sister has something against you,
leave your gift at the altar and go;
first be reconciled to your brother or sister,
and then come and offer your gift."*

Matthew 5:23-24

The only words that most of us had ever seen them exchange were shouts. At meetings, they never sat next to one another; they were always across from one another, as if in pre-meditated opposition. Across the table, they challenged one another, insulted one another, and accused one another of various misdeeds.

One Sunday, during the 'Passing of the Peace', as members of the congregation greeted one another with 'signs and words of the Peace of Christ', one of the men worked his way through the crowd to the seat of the other. They stood face to face. Neither smiled. They kept their hands at their sides. The one who had traversed the sanctuary, his red face appearing to cork an eruption from within, almost spat the word: "*Peace*". Then he inhaled, as if thinking what to say next. "And I have nothing more to add." His lips firmly pressed together, he did an about-face, and marched back to his own seat.

At the height of East-West political tensions of the 1980s, Prime Minister Margaret Thatcher met the then Soviet leader Mikhail Gorbachev. Following this, the first meeting between the two cold warriors, she was asked her impression of Mr Gorbachev. Her now famous response: "We can do business together." No gushing compliments. No tearful renunciations of past policies. No warm hugs. In fact, she continued by saying, "We both believe in our own political systems. He firmly believes in his; I firmly believe in mine. We are never going to change one another…" Nevertheless, there was the possibility that they could *do business*. (4)

Perhaps sometimes the reconciliation Jesus spoke of is just the willingness to agree to do business with the one whose actions we have, up until that point, detested. Nowhere does Jesus link reconciliation to warmth, to a smile, to a good feeling, to gushing apologies. Perhaps the walk across the sanctuary, a terse word through the teeth, is all we can manage. And faith is trusting that the exchange wasn't in vain.

"Don't lazily slip back into those old grooves of evil,
doing just what you feel like doing...
let yourselves be pulled into a way of life shaped by God's life...
love one another as if your lives depended on it..."

I Peter 1:13-25 (*The Message*)

He had not come forward for communion in almost a year. Why, we had asked. *Anger,* he said. Disillusioned with *people who call themselves Christians. Confused* by the behaviour of other church members, he said. They can do what they want, he seethed, but I'm not going to join them up there at the altar.

Misunderstandings and slights lurk just below the surface of intercultural community life. With little effort, a careless generalization, an unguarded slur, a whispered criticism, an unexamined double-standard can reach through the pleasantries and pull a victim under. And he had remained submerged for nearly twelve months. Friends extended a hand, offered an ear. He would just shake his head.

To his credit, he did not withdraw completely from the life of the community. He was there, a few weeks ago, cleaning up after the Christmas bazaar. He helped the congregation distribute groceries and clothing in the neighbourhood. He helped ladle soup to passers-by on Christmas Eve. He lifted his candle with the others that night as we had sung 'Silent Night'. Plenty of words had drifted his way during the season: *"do not fear... light shines in the darkness... home by another way..."*; but his face remained stoic. And come the Eucharist, his body stayed firmly planted in his seat.

More words on this January Sunday, but of a different tone. First Peter's call to holy living. Then Wesley's Renewal of the Covenant. Harsh directives from the eighteenth century cleric: *"search your hearts... renounce your own worthiness... your own wisdom... your own will... Consider what your sins are... be sure you are clear in these matters, do not lie to God... rely on God's promise... deny yourselves... renew the covenant... resolve to be faithful... with God's power, never go back... God, order my whole life according to your direction..."*

After the congregation prayed the famous covenant prayer together, *"put me to what thou wilt, rank me with whom thou wilt..."* it came time for Communion. The usual invitation was issued: *Christ invites all to his table...* They began to come forward, this odd collection of cultures and personalities, this thoroughly human Pentecost assembly. And among the some 400 outstretched hands awaiting the bread – amid the tensions unresolved, the conversations pending, the hurts not yet healed – two of them were his.

Together, by Acts of Grace

"E sia pace tra noi..." (may there be peace between us)

From the Italian translation of a Hebrew folk song

"I was actually a little scared to meet them," said the 14-year-old Israeli girl holding the guitar. The 15-year-old Palestinian boy sitting next to her smiled and pretended to clobber her with his flute. Five days ago the members of this musical ensemble – Jewish, Christian and Muslim – some from a Israeli school in Galilee and others from a Lutheran school in Bethlehem, had not known one another. It would be nearly impossible for them to meet in their homelands. However, through the work of Protestant churches in Italy, these children were selected to come to Milano, where they could meet. After arriving on separate flight, they met at the luggage carousel. "I was so surprised when one of them asked me if he could help me with my suitcase," said one girl.

Tonight's concert had been advertised as 'Notes of Peace'. Crowded into the fellowship hall, the young people played a mixture of Hebrew and Palestinian folk melodies. Guitar and saxophone, if a bit off-key, blended notes and rhythm. Photocopied sheet music was passed back and forth and followed attentively. In between two of the numbers, the Israeli teacher said sheepishly, "You will notice that we are still learning this music. We practised it separately, but we only began playing it together on Monday."

When it came time for questions, someone asked the group, "While you got to know one another this week, what surprised you about the other group?" The group stared at one another. The Palestinian Christian girl holding a recorder giggled. The Palestinian Muslim boy with the drum, sitting next to her, smiled and nudged the Christian Palestinian to say something. "The Israelis I met this week, they're all so kind," he said.

The boy holding the saxophone chimed in, "It's been important for me to know what they say about us, and what they really think about us."

One of the others nodded. "We've had some really interesting talks this week," she said, "What we are doing may seem like a little step, but for us, it is a very big step."

"I am sad because tomorrow we will all go home," said one of the girls, "they will go on one airplane, and we will go on another, and I don't know if we're going to see each other again."

It's late," said Palestinian teacher, "and our flights leave early tomorrow morning. Why don't you play one more song?" The Israeli girl with the trumpet held up a sheet: "What about this one?" The teacher agreed, and turned to the audience: "This last song is a traditional Palestinian welcome for a guest." The girl from Galilee stepped forward. And with a dip of the trumpet and no music in front of her, she led the group. Apparently, she had already learned these particular notes of peace by heart.

"Blessed are the merciful…"

Matthew 5:7

The teacher introduced the guest to the class. He had been a partisan during the Nazi occupation of Italy. He was a short man in his seventies with a pleasant face. He told the middle school children about living in the mountains and about listening to Radio London. He showed them his old food ration card. He spoke of the time he first saw Nazi and Italian fascist soldiers up close. "Their faces," he said, "had no light in them."

When the time came for questions, one boy asked, "Did you ever kill anyone?"

The man shook his head. "There was a time that I almost did. It was towards the end of the war. Our band of partisans had surrounded a barn. Most of the fascists had already escaped from it. But there were two men still hiding in there. We moved in closer, and the two fascists put their hands up. Some in our group started shouting at them. We all pointed our guns at them." He paused, as if to recall the scene.

"Then, we just decided that the war had gone on long enough. We knew it would be ending soon. These two guys had survived the whole war. Why kill them now? So we let them go. We just shouted at them to get out there."

"Twenty years later, I was in my apartment. My wife came in to tell me that I had some visitors. When I got to the door, there was a man about my age. He was standing there with a young woman. He said to me, 'We met in a barn at the end of the war. You spared my life. I just wanted to thank you… and to introduce you to my daughter.'"

"And I looked into that young woman's face," he said, "and I saw such light."

"When a wolf is together with other wolves, everything is fine. When a lamb is together with other lambs, everything is safe and sound. But if you put a wolf and a lamb together, inevitably something bad is going to happen. Some people are so disheartened by it that they give up the idea of integration altogether."

Eric H. F. Law (1)

In the car on our way home from a confirmation class trip, one of the teenagers from Ghana got a call on his cell phone. His eyes became wide with horror: *"Cosa!"* ("What!") he responded. *"Che e successo!"* ("What happened?").

His 19-year-old friend Abdul from Burkina Faso had been killed in Milano. Allegedly, young Abdul had entered a bar with a friend. The Italian owner saw him reach for a one-Euro package of biscuits on the counter, then leave the bar. The owner and his son ran him down in the street and beat him to death with a metal pipe.

The night after Abdul's murder, 7,000 people converged on Milano's Piazza Duomo. They lit candles, shouted angry chants, and hoisted banners which threatened retaliation. They marched to the bar, and in a gesture filled with meaning, placed one-Euro packages of biscuits on the ground outside the door. In the days leading up to his funeral, commentators and politicians on all sides weighed in with pronouncements. Abdul's parents made a quiet plea for justice, not revenge.

Lions and lambs living together, according to Eric Law, goes against our natural behaviours. Instinct would suggest everything to the contrary. Even if it is based on fear, leading separate lives would appear the more prudent, even the easier choice. On the other hand, sharing the same forest and living without fear seems virtually impossible. That week, God's peaceable kingdom sounded like an annoying, irrelevant bit of fantasy.

Our confirmation friend received a few other calls on his cell phone that week. The callers had not known Abdul, nor had they marched. Culturally speaking, they might appear to have more in common with the bar owners. But they had been at that confirmation retreat together. "Just calling to see how you're doing, *amico*," one of them said.

The God who inspired Isaiah's outlandish vision of wildlife cohabitation is the same God whose son compared the kingdom to tiny seeds.

"I am writing to you, little children…
I am writing to you, fathers
I am writing to you, young people…
Do not love the world or the things of this world."

I John 2: 12-15

This part of John's correspondence was directed to children, fathers and young people. But it appears he spent most of his words on the third group: the *figliolo* (young people). From what we can understand, these were not necessarily persons who were young in age, but also young in the faith. Perhaps John focused on them because they are the most vulnerable, their issues are not yet all sorted out, their feet not yet firmly planted in one camp or another. And they are still susceptible to the ways of the world, to the ways of, what John calls, "the evil one" .

One *figliolo* we know here in Milano is 18. He's Italian. He has grown up in a Christian home. He lives in an area that has been traditionally Italian but is changing, due to the influx of many foreigners. Most of his friends are Italian, but a few are foreigners. He's got a good heart. He's tolerant of others. But he has also seen some foreigners behave badly, even towards him, and he's got a good deal of anger towards some of them. But he knows other foreigners whom he likes. He's becoming an adult, and he could go either way – angry and racist, or welcoming and open. Time will tell.

Another *figliolo* we know here is also 18. He's not Italian. He has also grown up in a Christian home. Most of his friends share his nationality, but others are Italian. He's a good kid, with a good heart. But over the past two months he has witnessed fellow immigrants being beaten up, and heard of attacks on other foreigners. He's got a good deal of anger towards some Italians. But he knows some others whom he likes. He's becoming an adult, and he could go either way – angry and racist, or welcoming and open. Time will tell.

Both boys will have to choose from what John describes as the two "loves": towards the love of the world and its ways; or towards the love of God and God's ways – what John called "the new commandment". One way has little patience for the other person. The alternative way tries to honour the other person. Which way will these *figlioli* choose? A lot will depend on those of us around them, their fathers and brothers and aunts and uncles in the faith who can reinforce the good.

"He was despised and rejected by others;
a man of suffering and acquainted with infirmity;
and as one from whom others hide their faces he was despised,
and we held him of no account"

(Isaiah 53:3)

The volunteers always looked a little uneasy when Gerardo would enter. How would he be today? Often, we would hear him shouting before we ever saw him come down the stairs into the cafeteria. He would barge past the other guests, the frayed tails of the old grey trench coat flapping behind him, greasy strands of white, matted hair stuck to his forehead, and bits of yesterday's pasta still clinging to his beard.

He would storm to the front of the food line, demanding to get his *primo piatto* before anyone else. By some long unwritten exception to the rules, the cook would hand him his serving of *spaghetti con aglio*. Often, without a word of gratitude, Gerardo would grab the plate, then carry it towards his regular table. He would slam the plate on the table with such force that the sauce often spattered on the others seated at the table. No one liked sitting with him. He was loud, rude, and he smelled. More than once, volunteers would be called to clean up his plate that had toppled on the floor, or had been overturned on the table and left.

On more than one occasion Gerardo would stagger up to one of the volunteers, move close enough so that the toes of his mud-caked shoes would be touching theirs. His nostrils would flare, his eyes would raise with a kind of diabolical anger, his mouth would sneer. Others would be poised to intervene, and then in a gentle voice, he would say, "May I have another plastic fork, please?" Someone once spotted him in the train station. He was shuffling along a corridor, clutching a cup of coffee. He bent down next to a man sleeping on the pavement, slid the cup towards his head, then got up and walked away. Gerardo, whose namesake is the patron saint of falsely accused people, always had a way of confounding us.

And so, when before lunch one day, it was announced that Gerardo had died the night before, there was silence. Most people just shook their heads. "*Poverino,*" ("Poor guy") whispered one woman, "he was some mother's son."

On the day of his funeral, those who had served him meals, and those who had eaten meals side-by-side with him, gathered in the church. The smell of stale cigarettes and beer was almost as strong as the scent of holy incense. His casket was carried in by four nondescript city workers. When it came time for the prayers of intercession, one woman stood up and prayed, "O God, now Gerardo is being hugged by you. He is getting the hug that he wanted for so long, and never got."

> *"Grace: God's undeserved election of his people…*
> *a gift from God…*
> *consists of God giving himself to humankind…"*
>
> The Westminster Dictionary of Christian Theology (2)

Morning coffee is a ritual in Italy. The *brioches* come out of the oven any time after 6:30am, and the coffee machine runs non-stop all day. During morning and evening rush hour, all city bars are filled with clients, calling out requests to the bartender: *"Cappuccino!... Caffè macchiato!... Espresso!"* The protocol in some places is to drink the coffee, glance at the morning's paper, then pay on your way out. Other places ask that you pay at the cash register, take your receipt to the bar, and receive your order in return. In most places, regular customers can buy a 'subscription' of ten cups of coffee; in return for your loyalty, the bar awards you an eleventh one free.

One particular morning a young girl, probably in middle school, walked into the bar. It was still early, before the crowd, so the bartender waved to her from behind the bar. She waved back and walked over to the brioche rack. She picked up a paper napkin, moved her hand slowly above the selection, first over the chocolate-filled *cornetto*, then over to the *brioche con marmellata*, then eventually on one with cream. She daintily picked it up with the napkin, held it over her head for the bartender to see. He nodded and wished her a good day at school. She opened the door and left.

Another customer swung his head, widened his eyes, as if he had caught a petty theft in the act. He glanced over the bartender as if to make a citizen's arrest. The bartender gave him a dismissive wave and continued drying out the cups in front him.

Some prior transaction must have taken place, some previous agreement. The account had, apparently, all been paid. She merely needed to make her choice.

"Which of these three, do you think, was a neighbour?"

(Luke 10:37)

Four Ghanaian men were in the car together, driving back from a night prayer meeting at their church. As often happens in Italy, two police officers standing next to their parked squad car, waved them over. This was not a checkpoint for drunk drivers, but an immigration control stop. Police can ask for documents on the subway, in the bus station, in hospitals or school rooms. Some officers have been known to rip up the papers, denouncing them as fake. Others have been known to yell verbal abuse. Other such random checks have erupted in violence.

The four men became very nervous and whispered in Akan between them. Only the driver had proper immigration documents. One other was waiting for his to be processed. Another had recently been laid off from his factory job and, therefore, had lost his valid reason to stay in the country. The other was recently arrived. One *legale*, three *clandestini*.

The police officer strolled up to their car, rhythmically patting his baton on his open palm. He lowered his head and stared inside the car: "Documenti, per favore." The driver handed his *permesso di soggiorno* (permit of stay) to the officer, who studied it, jotted down some information on a small pad of paper, and handed it back.

"And the others?" he asked.

African men looked at one another and stared blankly at the officer. The driver, not sure what to say, began to explain that the group was returning from their church.

"Wait. Which church?" asked the officer.

"The Waldensian-Methodist Church" the driver responded.

"The one not too far from here?" the officer asked.

"Yes, that is our church."

"Ah, I know it… You're OK. Move along."

"But I say to you that listen, love your enemies..."

Luke 6:27

Giovanna Reggiani's body was found near a train station near her home in Rome. Evidence showed that she had been sexually assaulted before being murdered. It emerged that her murderer was a Rom (gypsy) man from a nearby shanty town. The next day the police swooped into the lot and rounded up hundreds of dwellers of the camps. Many of them – most were Romanian – were deported from the country. The government began deliberations about razing the entire makeshift village.

Anti-immigrant sentiment, already simmering, hit a boiling point. Politicians cited recent studies that suggest that foreigners commit a disproportionate number of crimes in Italy. Only a week prior to the murder, immigration statistics had shown that Romanians were now the largest foreign nationality represented in Italy. The mayor of Rome had reported that 75 percent of all arrests in his city involved Romanians. The day after the murder, spontaneous rallies sprouted up all over the city. People carried placards with words such as *Ora basta – Italia agli Italiani* (Enough already – Italy for the Italians). A billboard poster showed the face of a Native American chief, with the words: "The Indians were not able to stop immigration – now they live on reservations."

Days after the assault, a gang of vigilantes with clubs and knives beat up several Romanian men in a parking lot. During a Seria A soccer match that weekend, Lazio fans whistled in disrespect every time the Romanian star of the opposing team touched the ball. A political leader from the far right, who was calling for 20,000 more expulsions of Romanians from Rome, was cheered as he entered a television studio. Aboard a train in Florence later that week, a well-dressed Italian businessman observing the police dragging an immigrant woman down the platform, was heard to mutter, "*Meno male*" (roughly translated as "Thank heaven").

The front pages of the national newspapers featured photos of Giovanna's husband at her funeral, placing a red rose on her coffin. Another paper printed photos of the vacant lot where she had been assaulted. Still another, a mug shot of the presumed assailant. (Buried on page ten of one paper was an article about an unrelated incident in which a retired *Italian* army captain suffering from depression opened fire on a crowd from his apartment balcony – one person was killed and 17 injured). One paper dispatched a journalist to the suspect's Roma village of Avrig in Romania, where he interviewed former neighbours.

"That bastard?" recalled one of the townspeople, "He was in and out of prison even when he was here. He has brought great dishonour on all of us. So many of us have relatives in Italy. They're trying to make a better life for themselves and some kind of future for their children. You Italians have always been good to us. Why change that because of him?"

Giovanna Reggiani had been a Sunday school teacher in the Waldensian Church of Rome. At her funeral, the moderator of the Waldensian-Methodist Church of Italy called for justice but not retribution. The Sunday after the tragedy, a banner from the previous week's conference on Martin Luther King, Jr. still hung outside the church, with the words, *Dall'incubo puo nascere un sogno* (A dream can be born from a nightmare). In worship that day the pastor made a plea to the city for "no violence in the name of Giovanna." One of Giovanna's fellow Sunday school teachers met with the children of their class. "Giovanna will not be here with us anymore. But she is with God," she said. She then led the children in an exercise in which they were to pat one another on the back, then increase the force a bit, then even more. Before long, these blows were causing pain. "This," she said, "is what can happen when violence is allowed to escalate." The young people talked about their former teacher, about immigrants, about Romanians, about crime, and about the role of the church. At the end, one of the teenagers said, "Perhaps one way we could help make the world better would be to invite a Romanian to dinner."

A year later Giovanna Reggiani's family established a fund in her memory to provide schooling for Roma children.

Together, Step by Step

*"I do not call you servants any longer...
but I have called you friends..."*

John 15:15

Italian grammar lesson on subject pronouns: '*Tu*', called the *familiar form* of 'You', is used in the family, among intimate friends and fellow students, or when speaking to children, servants or animals. '*Lei*', called the *polite form* of 'You', is used when speaking to strangers, superiors, and people one is not well acquainted with.

English speakers and those of us who come from lands marked by what one foreign visitor to America called, "the lack of any sort of officialism in personal relations," find the distinction between the *familiar* and the *polite* hard to grasp. One misused pronoun can cause offence by being either sounding overly familiar or aloofly formal. For example, if you have accidentally stepped on someone's toe on the subway, you would use "*mi scusi*" if you had never met them, but "*scusami*" if you'd stepped on an acquaintance. Often, in a split-second, one has to assess social status, age, and the level of a friendship. What form do you use, for example, when your teacher is younger than you? What about when you've made friends with someone who is older than you? What if you see a respected person – your employer, your priest, an older person - every day? When does polite become familiar? When does a superior become an equal? How do you know if you are among *intimate* friends?

The rules get a bit simpler in the Christian community, but only a bit. For one thing, all prayers refer to God in the familiar: "Our Father, who art – *tu sei* – (as a child would lovingly address a parent) in heaven..." Early on we learned that in the Protestant church, the Italians use the *tu* form with one another, regardless of age. After all, as one person corrected our overly formal way of speaking to him. "*Per favore*, we're all brothers and sisters in Christ; there's no need to stand on pretences. Please use the '*tu*'."

Ah, but in practice, it's not so simple. What do you do when people conditioned to using the formal with each other *outside* the church, are members of the same community of faith? Many of the foreigners in this congregation clean homes of Italians. They are accustomed to a relationship of employer and servant. It's not easy to break the habit of addressing all Italians with a "*si, Signora*"... "*no, Signore*." Before worship one Sunday, an Italian woman mildly scolded a Filipino woman, because the Filipina had used the *Lei* form to address her. "Look," the Italian woman said, "we have known each other in this church for more than ten years. Why do you continue to use *il formale* with me? We are friends!"

The Filipino woman responded, "Well, I don't really know. I just call *You* – I mean, *you* – that way. I just do it without thinking." "But," the Italian sister responded, "if I continue to use the *tu* with you, and you continue to use the *Lei* with me, how can we ever be sisters in the church?"

Not long ago, during a council meeting discussion, the president sat at the head of the table. Beside him sat some of the other members, Italians. At the other end of the table sat several of the non-Italian members. The president talked for a while, then acknowledged the hand of one of the foreigners at the end of the table. "Mi scusi, Mauro," she began. "I mean, scusami, Mauro." And in the tentative shift of tense, polite became a little more familiar, and a community of superiors and inferiors, ever so slightly, more like intimate friends.

"Now, the woman was a Gentile, of Syrophoenician origin…"

Mark 7:26 (24-30)

A discussion around a Bible-study table of
modern-day Syrophoenicians

I like that Jesus had time to talk with a woman.

And she was a woman in need! Her daughter was sick.

I like that Jesus talked with an outsider.

If Jesus was a Jew, and this woman was a… my Bible says pagan, what language did they speak with each other? Maybe one of them had to speak the other's language?

No, they would have spoken Aramaic, right?

How do we know that? They came from two different cultures.

Well, which ever, I like it that Jesus seemed to have his mind all made up. I mean, about who was in the kingdom and who was out, who would receive his blessing and who would not. And then he meets this foreign woman and she convinces him to change his mind.

Even Jesus changed his mind?

Well, didn't he? At first he didn't seem to think she deserved to have her daughter healed. He compared her people to dogs! But when she said "yes, but even the dogs need to eat the crumbs from under the table," he told her he liked her faith. He healed her daughter.

Yes, you could say that she evangelized him.

Evangelized? How do you evangelize Jesus?

Maybe Jesus was still learning. She was learning, and he was learning. After she spoke with Jesus, he was an even better Messiah.

It makes you wonder who might evangelize us if we let them.

"When diversity starts to get lived out, however well or poorly,
folk in the church begin to see how demanding it is.
Diversity costs. It costs spiritually, it costs emotionally,
it costs economically…"

Emilie Townes (1)

Two of our neighbours fell in love. That is, in love with each other. They were neighbours first. They lived in adjacent apartments on the same floor. They would see each other frequently. They would chat in the elevator. So, I suppose, they would do things like neighbours do: "May I borrow your ladder?" "Do you have an extra egg?" "I made a little too much soup – would you like a bowl?" However it happened, one thing led to another and they became more than just neighbours.

Last week, one of them came to apologize for construction noise that we would be hearing all week. "You see, we have decided to build a door between our apartments. We just decided that we had had enough crossing the hallway to see each other. Now we will be sharing a space. We're really not changing too much inside our apartments, but we're connecting them. Neither one of us was ready to give up our apartment. I mean, we're middle-aged, we both have our lives and our habits, but we decided it was time to connect them."

I felt like telling them that we, in our multi-ethnic congregation, were trying to do something similar.

The day of the construction, we heard the pounding. Apparently, the wall between the two apartments was not too flimsy. It took two men with sledgehammers and another with a jackhammer to break through 40-year-old mortar. They carried several wheelbarrows full of bricks and cement chips outside.

The next day we saw a salesman arrive. He was carrying several wood trim corners, presumably choices for the new door frame. This would not be an open passageway; there would be a door that could be opened and closed. But what kind of door would it be? Seems like that detail had not yet been decided.

The next day painters came. Several plastic pails with several different colours of paint appeared in the hallway. Apparently, the door was not going to be the only change. Perhaps the door between the two apartments had made each inhabitant reconsider the interior of their own place. Doors can do that. An open door can allow light into a previously dark room. Who knows what smudges became suddenly visible, how the open door made a colour take on an unfamiliar tint.

The following day we could hear the scrape, thud, and squeak of table legs and dressers skidding across the floor. Not only were the two apartments connected now, but some sharing and rearranging was occurring. Can't put things in the space where there is now a door. Lengthy wall space, and perhaps some other things, are lost.

I'd like to know when the door is open and when it is closed. Is it ever locked? Will a knock always precede its opening? Will it ever be slammed shut? Will it ever be opened by a trembling hand, a remorseful voice? What will be kept the same in each apartment?

For that matter, will the adjoining apartments have a common thermostat, or will they maintain separate room temperatures? Will the door ever be propped open for the cross-breeze that could not have happened before? And – OK, this is a little picky – but who's paying for the new door?

Lots of things to be decided. Cohabitation, I suppose is not as simple as merely installing a door. Living in community never is.

"People get tired... people get tired..."

Martin Luther King, Jr. (2)

Priests, nuns, social workers, government officials, representatives from charitable organizations had all packed the hall. Every year in October they gather in this same building to hear the new statistics on immigration in Italy. The meeting is part convention, part networking, part continuing education, part reunion, part strategy session. However, the chatting and laughter stops when the statistics are distributed. Still hot from the copy machine, their arrival has a sobering impact. As hard as we may be working to address the needs of immigrants, they are arriving on Italian soil at a higher rate each year. The related problems don't get any easier: resources spread more thinly, health-system more over-burdened, frustrations more raw, and everyone more tired.

Perhaps intentionally, the first speaker addressed the issue of weariness of *accoglienza* (welcome), noting the trend in different countries in Europe: for example, after the bombing of the London Underground; after the riots in the *banlieu* of Paris. Many people are less patient about issues of integration. People on all sides of the issue – those trying to enter a new society, those trying to make space for them, and those who resent their arrival – are experiencing what the speaker called *la fatica di integrazione* (integration fatigue).

Our congregation seems to be battling a bad case of integration fatigue these days. "Enough of this bilingual worship!" shouted one member in frustration. "Let's go back to everything being in Italian, like it always was!" Later he apologized: "I guess I'm just tired of all the complications." A similarly frustrated foreign member recently threatened: "Why don't we just split off and have our own church!" And they are just the more vocal ones.

"Fatigue," the speaker continued, "is a natural result of doing this hard work. Integration is, after all, not a job that is ever finished. It is *un percorso lungo* (a long journey). And on the journey, fatigue is bound to creep in." She glanced up from her notes and added, "But I'm looking out at a standing-room-only crowd this morning. Your presence here," she said, "says that we have not given up."

Few quick victories in this game. Often feels like more setbacks than glories. Faith, though, is the long perseverance, or as one person has written, "a long obedience in the same direction."

"Brothers and sisters, do not be weary in doing what is right."
2 Thessalonians 3:13.

"…you who were once far off have been brought near"

Ephesians 2:13

The Parco Pubblico in Affori, outside Milano, sits on the former property of the Villa Litta Modigliani. The villa is still there, although it now serves as a community centre. The rolling hills around the building are dotted with soccer goals and fitness bars. *Nonnas* walk their grandchildren and young couples cuddle on benches. A buzz of Spanish, Arabic, Mandarin and Italian fills the air.

Towering above the activities in the park are very elegant, very old trees. Their placement is symmetrical enough to suggest that someone, centuries ago, measured the distance between them. They are senior citizens of a planned community, which now bears no resemblance to the terrain when they were all saplings.

The circumference of several of them is so wide that it might take the entire backfield of the nearby soccer team, hands locked together, to wrap around the trunk. The diameter of one tree in particular is unusually large. On second glance, however, it is obvious that this tree was once two trees, which, over time, merged together. They were probably never intended to be together. As seedlings, they may have once been seven or eight feet apart. But as they reached heavenward over the years, their torsos expanded, touched, and eventually merged. Spring after spring, ring after ring, the two trees pressed in on each other. Their bark became common. The two have become one. No daylight shows between them until a good 15 feet off the ground, where they bend slightly away from each other, and resume their climb, only slightly separated.

The ancient Byzantines used intertwining Cypress trees in their Christian iconography. In some images the cross was adorned with a pattern of vines which reached out to become the roots of trees on either side of the cross. Like two inhabitants of the same forest – introduced, betrothed and joined in a life no longer as individuals.

The united tree quietly observes as soccer players dispute a call, as two strangers sharing the same bench strain to communicate, as lovers bicker and reconcile.

Time passes. Seasons come and go. Imperceptibly, mysteriously, molecules of bark extend, new leaves sprout, and a ring is added.

"Then I will draw near to you for judgment;
I will be swift to bear witness against the sorcerers,
against the adulterers, against those who swear falsely,
against those who oppress the hired workers in their wages ..."

A reading from Malachi 3:5:

The tall African man standing at the microphone in the front of the Synod assembly suddenly stopped reading. Silence. Delegates in the hall began to crane their necks to see what had happened. Had he lost his place? Had the breeze blown a page?

The service had been organized in a hurry to protest against a set of new laws that discriminate against foreigners. For the past 24 hours the Waldensian-Methodist press office had made contact with key newspapers and local television news networks. Computer experts had compiled a series of images of immigrants to flash on a big screen during the vigil. Several people had hand-painted posters. Archivists had gathered articles detailing injustices to be read aloud. Hundreds of people – most of them European, and most of them middle class – had entered the church that morning for the vigil. More than one had glanced at the television cameras and adjusted a shirt collar.

Ten people had taken their turn at the microphone, reading selected scripture verses about how to treat the alien: from Leviticus, from the Gospels, from Ephesians, etc. The liturgy was moving along as planned, properly choreographed and well-executed. And then it was his turn. He introduced the scripture, began reading, and then stopped. After a long, uncomfortable silence, he brought his hand up to his face and rubbed his eyes. The quick inhale of a sob came through the microphone. He shook his head and walked back to his seat.

A young pastor dropped her chin to her chest. A cameraman flicked the off-switch on his video recorder. One of the organizers closed her folder, found a Bible, flipped to Malachi, walked up to the microphone, and read the rest of the verse:

"...the widow and the orphan, against those who thrust aside the alien,
and do not hear me, says the Lord of hosts."

And then she sat down. And in the even longer, unscheduled silence that followed, something felt turned-off, and something else turned on.

"Where is the one who is wise?"

I Corinthians 1:20

"I was sitting with my *signore* a few months before he died," she said. I often sat with him when my other work around the house was finished. His wife would be at work, and sometimes it was just the two of us sitting there in the lounge. We would talk. He would ask some things about the Philippines, about my family." She paused and blinked her eyes in a tired way. "He was very ill then, but he was still very smart.

"I think all my cleaning was done for that day. Maybe I was helping him answer his correspondence. I would sometimes do that, because it was hard for him to open envelopes and all. He had a lot of correspondence because he had been a writer. I think a very well-known writer, but I am not sure.

"This particular day, he said something that surprised me. He said, "*Sono triste*" ("I am sad").

"Sad, *signore*? I said to him. I mean, he was an important writer. He lived in this beautiful apartment."

"Yes, Ann, I am sad. I want to ask you something."

"Yes, *signore*?"

"What do you do when you are sad?"

"Me, *signore*? You are asking *me*? I mean, he wanted to ask *me* what *I* do when I'm sad!"

"Yes," he said to me, "please tell me."

"Well… *signore*. I try to remember to think of the blessings in my life. There are really so many things if you stop and think about it. I pray, too. Yes, I pray. I also try to remember happy memories. Those help me feel happy."

"And do you know what he said to me, pastor? He said, 'Anne, you are a very wise woman'. Me! He is the writer, and he was calling me wise? I said, 'Signore, you are the wise one'. But he said, 'No, you are the one who is wise'."

"…you are accepted in spite of the fact of being unacceptable"

Paul Tillich (3)

Like hell you're accepted!
Do you think Jesus wants you to stay the way you are?

Critique of Tillich, attributed to Stanley Hauerwas (4)

It was hard to detect approval or criticism from the conductor's face. Once he had ascended to his platform, he concentrated on the pages before him. This was probably not his usual assignment. On the risers behind the Orchestra of Padova and Venezia stood 25 children from Milano's City Children's Choir (our daughter was one of them).

From the initial tap of his baton on the music stand until the final note of Pippo Molino's 'Angelus', he looked intently at adult musicians and adolescent singers alike. He would motion to the balding first violinist, then to the heavy-set cellist, then to the pimply sopranos and pony-tailed contraltos. With the tales of his black tuxedo flapping behind him, he thrashed his way through the difficult piece.

Although he knew his musicians well, he had not trained this young choir. The practice sessions had been led by his acolytes. Except for one, brief dress-rehearsal, this was his first extended time with the combined orchestra and youth choir. So, it was not easy to decipher what relationship, if any, he had with his adolescent choristers. Although certainly no teddy bear, his promptings were done in a way not unkind. Was he suffering the little children to sing unto him, or suffering from the little children singing under him? Hard to tell.

With perspiration covering his forehead, the Maestro led them through the final stanzas, thrusting both his arms down to conclude the piece. Then he stretched them out straight, as if to make sure that the applause was shared by each musician and singer.

He stepped off his dais and walked to the back of the stage, where the choir members were beginning to file down the stairs. Putting himself at the base of the steps, he looked at each young person as they descended. From where we were sitting, it sounded as if he were making the sound of a snake, *ssss…ssss…ssss…ssss*. His facial expression revealed no clues.

Later, I asked our daughter what he had said to each of them.

"Oh," she said, "He was saying, '*Siete bravissi-missi-missi-missi-missi-mi*' ('You are magnifi-nifi-nifi-nifi-nifi-cent!'). '*Ma potete migliorare*' ('But you can do better')."

"Was that a compliment?" I asked.

"Um," she responded, "I'm not sure."

The Master's emphasis, somewhere between acceptance and challenge, is not quite clear.

*"How very good and pleasant it is
when kindred live together in unity!"*

Psalm 133:1

Bi-lingual worship, we are discovering, is not a precise science. Long explanations, puzzled looks and clapping out of rhythm are all part of an awkward courtship. People still sit in their favourite spots. Neighbours whisper to one another in their native tongues. Old friends sit with old friends. Aisles still separate. Dual translations can both unify and divide. Like a tapestry in progress, the community's seams are plainly visible.

One Sunday, as the leaders laboured through the announcements, Giovanni was sitting at the back of the sanctuary. With both hands he held a toddler, who was delighting in gripping the old man's bifocals. Giovanni playfully lifted the child over his head, then would look up and grin. Then he would bring the boy lower, nuzzling his nose into the child's belly. When the little one would giggle, Giovanni's eyes would widen with mock chagrin. He would shush him gently. Things would quiet, and then up he'd go again. Although I couldn't see the child's face, it was clear that he was enjoying himself at least half as much as was Giovanni. Through six announcements, a hymn, one long prayer for unity (in Italian and English), the Lord's Prayer, another hymn, and into the benediction, they smiled at one another. *Go in peace to love God and serve your neighbour. Amen.* The man hugged the child, as a grandfather embraces a grandson, as if congratulating him on some mutual achievement.

After worship, I asked him, "Giovanni, that child you had on your lap. Who is he?"

"Oh him?" he said. "I'm not sure whose child he was. One of the Filipino sisters gave him to me to hold."

Together, through *Carità*

"…your people will be my people…"

Ruth 1:16

They are a long way from their home in the northern province of the Philippines. 'Inolda', the mother of the family, her husband and their young son have been living in Milano for years. Later, when Inolda's sister, brother-in-law and two girls came to Italy, the only work the two parents could find was as live-in domestic helpers to two different elderly persons living outside Milano. Neither employer would allow the girls to live on the premises. But since it meant having work, they figured out a solution. Through some negotiations and moving of furniture, Inolda and her husband agreed to let their two nieces live with them. This living arrangement meant that five persons shared a two-room apartment, kitchen and bathroom.

We occasionally bump into Inolda in the neighbourhood. "Buon giorno, ciao, Inolda, what are you up to today?" "Oh, one of the girls is sick today and we need to keep her home from school. I'm just coming back from the pharmacy with some medicine the doctor prescribed for her him." Often we see the girls, hand in hand with their little nephew. We're not even sure he understands the formal distinctions of family. When we've been in their home, the girls hang on their aunt as if she were their mother. She lovingly tussles their hair and even reprimands them just as if she were. She reminds them not to forget their lunches in the morning, she prepares snacks for them when they get home, she sees to it that they're doing their homework. All this while both she and her husband also hold down their own domestic jobs, trying to make enough to feed everyone in the household.

The search for a better living overseas changes many family configurations. Aunts become mothers. Uncles, fathers. Nieces, daughters. Cousins, brothers and sisters. At first glimpse, it is sad to know that parents are not with their children, to see their daily growth, to be with them through the tough days and the celebrations. And yet, many of the church people we have come to know offer hospitality to their relatives and friends in a casual way that doesn't reveal a conscious choice. It seems more like the natural thing to do for someone in need – another plate prepared, another mattress set out. Christian ethicists talk about cultivating habits of Christian living, so that something like radical hospitality no longer look extraordinary, even when it is.

*"…when you give something to a needy person,
do not make a big show of it…"*

Matthew 6:2 (Good News Translation)

The older gentleman is something of a fixture in our neighbourhood. He shuffles along the sidewalks, rests on park benches, stops for long periods to look at shop window displays. The top of his bald head is dirty. The long wisps of white hair that dangle to his shoulders are usually matted and greasy. His trousers (I think he alternates between two pairs) are stained. The leather thongs in his sandles, which he wears even in the winter, are torn. When the weather turns cold, he dons an old dark green military-issue overcoat, frayed at the bottom.

It would appear that he is too old to work. Nor does he seem to have any family in the area. He is always on his own. Well, not quite.

When we first started to notice him, we wondered how he managed to live. Over time, however, we have seen him in different shops around our street. One day, when we walked into a café, he was sitting at the back table, slowly forking through a plate of pasta. Not long after, we noticed him stepping out of the tailor's next to the reggae record shop. With his hands he was lifting up a baggy sweater by each shoulder as he glanced down to see how it was fitting over his frame. We've seen the grocer hand him a two-litre bottle of water.

These exchanges are usually silent. I've never heard the man mutter a word. Nor have I ever overheard any verbal interaction involving the charity. Quietly, the man receives what he needs.

Not long ago, I walked into the bread store. There he was, standing up by the counter, holding an empty plastic sack. As I entered, the baker was shaking his head. "No sir," whispered the baker to man, "maybe not that one today. You had that yesterday. How about some *foccaccia* with some good vegetables on top…like this one with some zucchini?"

The man nodded. The baker wrapped up the *foccaccia* with zucchini, and handed the bag across the counter. "Next customer? Whose next, please? Good morning, signora!"

"Freely you have received, freely give."

Matthew 10:8, (adapted)

"When I arrived in Italy 25 years ago, I was a young woman. I had never been out of my village. My new husband had said to me, "There is nothing for us here. We must leave Africa. So, we came here. I knew no one. We had one child and I was also pregnant. I didn't speak the language. And only some months after we got here, my husband left me. There were two children then, and me.

What was I going to do? I knew no one. I cried and cried. I didn't like it here. Without a husband, what would I do? I wanted to return to my people, my village. I began to think of my church life back home. Oh, I missed it very much. And I thought to myself, *I must find a church.*

Someone told me of the English-speaking congregation in the city. I went there. I sat in the back. I could sing again. They said it was OK to come there. They said I could bring the children. I stayed at that church. They gave me encouragement. My church kept me from giving up. My church gave me strength. I did not go back to Africa. I stayed here. Aha! Now I am on the *concistoro* (church council). I guess they think I can contribute something to them."

As our train showed signs of slowing, she began to pack up her things. "Tonight is one of my nights to help."

"Help? What kind of help?" I asked.

"Each Tuesday I help the group feed the refugees. Do you know that we make 400 *panini*? Oh, so much bread, and *formaggio* and *prosciutto*. Sometimes we give them *tonno*, you know, tuna. We put in boxes of fruit juice and some fruit, too. We find where the refugees are – usually we go near the train station. I also know the buildings where they often stay. We go there. Usually, we have no sandwiches left at the end of the night.

"We tell them about a place where they can come. The church is not far, we say. It has a lounge, with chairs to sit. The men can shave. They can watch television, even CNN. Some people come in the summer months, but in the winter, many people come to be in the warm air for several hours. Last Friday, I met a woman there. She needed clothes for her husband. I will check in my apartment to see if my son has any trousers that he no longer wears. And I will bring them with me tomorrow morning. I think she will be there tomorrow morning."

*"...and he sent them out to proclaim the kingdom of God
and to heal."*

Luke 9:2

In 1861, as a 30-year-old pastor, Henry James Piggott left his home in England to come to Italy. Together with another pastor by the name of Richard Green, and a former Catholic seminarian named Benedetto Lissolo, he was sent by the British Methodist Missionary Society at a significant time in Italian history. According to church historian Giorgio Tourn, their commissioning coincided with the impression in Britain that "Italy was already moving toward a religious revitalization, biblically inspired, that went parallel to the national Risorgimento (Unification)."

Piggott, the son of a missionary family, was supported by well-meaning people who were convinced that Italian 'papists' were poor pagans to be converted. Piggott, however, had a divergent sense of God's mission. He had no intention of imposing a foreign model of the church, like British Methodism, on the Italians. In fact, even today, Italian Methodists still remember how, while working in the northern town of Ivrea, Piggott's activities attracted people to the message of the Gospel. Yet, if someone came closer to Christ, Piggott would contact one of the Protestant pastors (there were Waldensians and Free Church communities in the area at the time), and encourage them to offer pastoral care to this new convert. One of our Italian colleagues reflected, "While future pastors would be more concerned with building up a Methodist structure in Italy, Piggott was not into that. You could compare him to Jesus and the other missionaries to Paul. Don't get me wrong: there needed to be a Paul to make the church what it is today. But first there needed to be the message."

However, much like the Wesleyan movement, Methodism in Italy did begin to adopt a structure. The first Methodist Conference in Italy was held in 1868. In Milano and later in Padua, Piggott helped set up a home for girls. In the face of widespread illiteracy, he and others helped establish schools connected with the Methodist chapels. The majority of the members came from humble backgrounds – workers, artisans, small shopkeepers – a reflection of the demographics of the early Italian Methodist movement. Even with his dynamic leadership, Piggott seemed to have a longer-range vision. Convinced that leadership for the Methodist movement must come from within, Tourn notes that "Piggott always had at heart the training of ministers..." (1)

Piggott died in 1917 at the age of 86, having lived almost two-thirds of his life in his adopted country of Italy. He was buried in Rome, where, on his gravestone are written these words:

Henry James Piggott

Minister of the Gospel of Christ
who laboured in Italy for 56 years,
sowing the good seed of faith
in many hearts.
Following in his Master's steps,
he went about doing good.

"Let the same mind be in you that was in Christ Jesus,
who though he was in the form of God,
did not regard equality with God as something to be exploited,
but emptied himself, taking the form of a slave,
being born in human likeness.
And being found in human form, he humbled himself
and became obedient to the point of death –
even death on a cross."

Philippians 2:5-8

Guido is a man of few words. He serves at his parish's soup kitchen. Every time he hands someone a plate of food, he does a little nod. Guests know that he is the most lenient waiter. If you want seconds, ask Guido; he's the softy.

He has attended mass nearly every day of his 79 years. I didn't hear that from him, though. One of his friends told me.

Whenever we leave the building, he briefly touches the crucifix near the door and whispers something.

"Guido," I said one day, "would you tell me what that means to you, the way you touch the crucifix like that?"

"Oh that?" He smiled, then shrugged.

"The feet, I touch our Lord's feet. The least respectful part of the body. Dirty, you know? He washed feet. He was the Master, the Rabbi, but he washed the disciples' feet. King of Kings, but he washed feet.

"When I'm doing it, I am praying for humility like that. See you next time, my brother."

Star of Wonder, Star of Bread

This doughy comet
made of flour and water,
is slightly burnt around its edges –
less from a rapid entry through the atmosphere,
than a tardy exit from the oven.
It must have fallen to earth
more than once,
knocked to the ground,
leaving a few crumbs on the tiles,
and that crack in its crusty tail;
then carefully restored to the heavens
above the wood stick manger,
over the clay sheep,
the burlap shepherds,
and the porcelain holy parents.
Some generous baker,
with floury hands, must have
molded, cut, and glazed with egg yolk,
until the incarnation was made
in the image of his guild;
then gave it to the congregation
that feeds people in this room.
Today several volunteers stare at it.
Kind of odd, no? asks one.
Gone stale, says another.
A guest arrives for lunch,
glances up at it
and smiles.
That must mark the place,
to find food, no?

Together, in the Spirit

"precarious: dependent on circumstances beyond one's control:
uncertain, unstable, insecure…
origin: (Latin) obtained by entreaty or mere favour, hence uncertain.
See PRAYER."

Precarious.
The plexiglass box,
once on solid pavement,
now rests beside a gaping chasm of
tangled wires and shards of brick.
This Telecom Italia booth
has withstood
many a jackhammer attack
on the surrounding asphalt;
but now,
the unfinished excavation
has it perched uneasily
above decaying layers
of post-war road rubble,
pre-war cobblestones,
and Roman terracotta drain pipes.
So it hovers,
this leaning shack,
on a thin layer of concrete,
above the concave abyss below.
One lonely cable
attached to its roof,
seems to hold the whole thing
from tumbling into the chaos.
Would the rattle of a passing bus
topple it over,
into the hole?
Exposed and fragile,
It awaits a caller.
Does it still function?
Is it still connected?
Can you hear me?
Preghiera.

"You are my beloved, and on you my favour rests"

Matthew 3:17 (adapted)

Visitors to Milano often comment on the graffiti. It's everywhere: caricatures, threats, political statements, gang tags, indecipherable scribbling, elabourate puff lettering, soccer team taunts, colourful profanities (with diagrams), and once in a while – a love note.

We saw one such note on the wall of a train station in the northern town of Pinerolo. Someone had painted in broad white brush strokes: TI AMO, PRINCIPESSA! (I love you, princess!). It looks like it was meant to greet the recipient on her arrival at the station. Did she see it? If so, did she know who it was from?

The line comes from Roberto Benigni's film *La Vita e Bella*. Benigni's character falls in love with a woman, played by his real-life wife Nicoletta Braschi. In the small village where they live, he keeps bumping into her. Each time he greets her with the same words. Throughout all the seasons of their romance – the joys and the tragedies – he keeps calling her his *principessa*.

Not long after the first sighting, we saw the same message, with the same thick white lettering, along a roadway near Firenze. Wow, we thought, that guy (and his *principessa*) really get around. Prone to wander as she is, he is equally persistent in professing his love.

Yet again, in the southern town of Cisterna, we have seen the same graffiti. This time, the artist seemed even more intent on getting his message to his beloved. It shouts from the overpass entering town, on each of the two stop signs at the first main intersection, on the back of a park bench, and then on each of the 16 arrow markers signalling a curve in the road. Pretty hard to miss. By now we were even more curious: who is this beloved *principessa*? Didn't she believe him the first time? The guy certainly is persistent. But apparently, she needed to hear it more than once.

Henri Nouwen once preached on the words Jesus heard after his baptism. "I want you to hear that voice, too," Nouwen told his listeners. "It is a very important voice that says,

> 'You are my beloved son; you are my beloved daughter. I love you with an everlasting love. I have moulded you together in the depths of the earth. I have knitted you in your mother's womb.

I've written your name in the palm of my hand and I hold you safe in the shade of my embrace. I hold you. You belong to Me and I belong to you. You are safe where I am. Don't be afraid. Trust that you are the beloved...'" (1)

We're on the lookout for the love-struck paint brusher's next message. Maybe, instead of wondering who it is for, we can claim it for ourselves.

"For the darkness shall turn to dawning,
and the dawning to noon day bright..."

Ernest Nichol (2)

The hand-written instructions are taped to the chapel railing in this Salesian Order Catholic Church: *The time for the night to change to dawn, to day time, to sunset and to night again is about five minutes; just the right amount of time to pray and reflect.*

On wooden platforms, villagers, animals, and palm trees surround the Christ child.

Camels and palm trees silhouette the background. Not-too-wondrous stars lend minimal light in the blackened sky. The miniature manger is in shadow. The timer hums, tucked beneath the tarp.

Hint of glories streaming from heaven afar, peek over the cardboard hillside. Dawn touches the face of an innkeeper, then a donkey, until the whole plain is aglow.

High noon comes at two and one-half minutes. Light glares off Jesus' porcelain cheeks. All is calm, all is bright, but only for a bit, before radiant beams begin to fade. The ticking from beneath the clay hillside sounds like impatient fingers on a table.

Sun sets on the day. Spotlights go dark. The cycle concludes and the heavenly scene resembles any other obscure village at night.

Five minutes to pray and reflect. Enough time to recall the shades of the story: light, darkness, pain, joy, fear and reassurance. Pain of birth. Joy of welcome. Fear in the fields. Reassurance from heaven.

Maybe some prayers only come out at night. Others need the promise of dawn. Some bask in midday clarity. Others need the promise that this day will dim.

God's timer clicks on.

Studying theology in England in the 1960's, Desmond Tutu noted that Western theologians "were looking for answers to questions that Africans were not asking...his fellow students were wrestling with how to minister in a society that, under the influence of scientific progress and of interpretations which denied the transcendent, was losing its belief in God." This was a relevant exercise for western Christians, Tutu said, but it was irrelevant for Africans: "Our people did not doubt that God existed..." (3)

'Being the church together', the catchy slogan used by the Italian Protestant churches for intercultural congregations, gets tricky, especially when talking about what we believe. Friendliness, shared meals, bi-lingual worship can draw us beyond the boundaries of our own cultures and lead us to a certain point of contact. But when we start discussing our faith, dialogue can become strained.

With this hurdle in mind, a multicultural group sat in a cold sanctuary one Saturday afternoon to discuss 'prayer, miracles, and healing'. In a rather frank assessment of the impact of the 1960s crisis of faith in the churches, one Italian admitted that many in his generation were a bit suspicious of prayer: after 2,000 years of prayer, is the world a better place? Do we really believe in prayer as some magic spell? Is it a Freudian deception that brings us some peace of mind, but no real results? If God knows everything anyway, why bother to pray? What about prayers for healings which never happen?

An African man crinkled his forehead and shook his head. "I know the Lord answers prayers. The Bible says, 'Pray without ceasing'. Each morning and each evening our family prays together. Because we know that God answers prayers."

One of his compatriots shook his head slowly: "I sometimes wonder if Italians have any faith at all. It's kind of sad to me."

"No!" interjected a young Italian man. "You can't say that. Just because we have some scepticism, it doesn't mean we have no faith!"

"I don't think it's because I lack faith," commented another European. "Sometimes, I just find it hard to pray. Don't have the words, or the time, or the space... I don't know."

"I have no difficulty in praying," said one immigrant woman. "I pray all the time. It's just is natural for me."

Another participant said, "I don't know if it has anything to do with being European or not. It's just not in my character to ask anyone for help. I guess that makes it hard for me to pray to God for anything."

How do people who have not known scarcity learn dependence? (As someone once noted, it is the people without health insurance who pray for miracles). How do Europeans, who emerged from the Holocaust contemplating the death of God, and who one contemporary theologian observes suffer from "metaphysical boredom," (4), attempt to converse with Africans, for whom "religion [is] more than just religion. It [is] an all-pervasive reality" (5). How can we quantify the air we have breathed? How do we measure the conversations we have heard, the knees under which we have sat, the songs we have sung, the perplexities unsolved, the joys, the sorrows, the life experiences on separate continents?

And what happens when one of us says to the other, "Let us pray"? As hands are clasped together or lifted high, heads bowed or raised, does one believer dismiss the other's prayer as naïve? Falsely pious? Simple? Inversely, does the other believer discount his neighbour's prayer as too rational? Agnostic? Pagan? Can the two pray at the same table? Could your words, your silences, your spirit complement what I lack?

The answer to questions like these will decide whether we are the church – not side by side – but together.

"What I whisper in your ears, shout from the housetops…"

Matthew 10:27 (New Living Translation)

Whenever we see an American movie on Italian television, it is dubbed. In other words, rather than hear the words of the original actors in English, we hear the voices of Italian actors. Same script, someone else's voice. Fine to get the words, but a pity not to hear Sean Connery's brogue, or Robert DeNiro's asking, "You tawkin' ta me?" While lips and words usually synchronize relatively well, it is much harder to convey content and emotion.

Last week, we watched 'Robin Hood, Prince of Thieves' on Italian television. The Italian dubbing, in this case, improved Kevin Costner's curious mid-western accent in Sherwood Forest. Little John knocks Robin into the river with a splash that translates well. Swords clang in either language. The Sheriff of Nottingham's sneers need no dubbing.

One of the most memorable audible lines of the film comes at the climactic battle to save the kingdom. As the evil Sheriff is forcing Maid Marian to marry him instead of her true love, Robin of Locksley, he sequesters her into one of the castle turrets, and commandeers a corrupt priest to marry them. Outside, the battle rages as Robin and his men attempt to storm the castle. In perhaps the movie's most memorable audio sequence, Mary Elizabeth Mastrantonio's Marian lets loose a blood-curdling scream: "ROBINNNNNNN!!!!!" It is a clip that has lived on in celluloid highlights.

Unfortunately, however, the Italian woman who read Marian's part does not put the necessary anguish behind that particular line. Rather, it sounds more like Marian was calling her love in for some lemonade that she'd just prepared on the veranda. Arrows fly! Swords clash! Music builds to a crescendo …and Marian wonders, if he is not too busy, Robin might, per chance, pay her a visit in the tower sometime.

I remember being in a church in South Africa. Our group of Americans had practised a rendition of 'Siyahamba' ('We are marching in the light of God'). We began to sing, but half-way through our somewhat pallid attempt at the song, the South African pastor jumped up. "Stop! Stop!" he cried out. "This song came out of the struggle against apartheid!" he protested. "This song was sung at the darkest hours of our faith! This song reminded us that even though we felt like we were in darkness, we were walking in the LIGHT of GOD! When we sing it, we dance in joy that the Lord is with us! Sing it like you mean it!"

When a lot is at stake, God calls forth from us not just our voices, not just our mouths, not even just the right words, but our passion.

"Advent is…the preparation for the coming One.
So, how to prepare? Clean the house.
Not just my residence, but the house of my soul."

John Parker (6)

The Nigerian woman, her hair wrapped in *kente* cloth, picked up the hymnals and Bibles and placed them on a chair. Then, with a red-handled broom, she slid two candy wrappers and a crumpled up Bible tract across the aisle. She gently tapped the shoulder of a man seated near the pulpit, and he promptly scooted his chair over. She pointed to a purse on the floor; a woman seated nearby lifted it up to make way for her broom. All this *during* worship.

All over Italy, small Protestant congregations such as this one share facilities with other small Protestant congregations. So, on Sundays, the closing benediction of one often gives the signal for the other faithful to enter. Groups meet in the doorway, one exiting while the other enters. This sister, with Martha-like intensity, was doing her part of hospitality: leaving the place clean for the next group.

Sweep, sweep. A girl lifted her little brother's baby chair. Sweep, sweep. The sweeper scanned the floor, apparently content, and sat back down. The pastor began wrapping up his sermon. Martha jumped up again, having noticed some coloured pencils on the floor in the row ahead of her. She nudged the woman in front of her and pointed; the woman obediently reached down to retrieve them. Sweep, sweep. The broom bumped my feet. I lifted them, not without being a little perturbed. Couldn't the cleaning wait until a less holy time? Final hymn. More sweeping. She handed the dustpan to one of the brothers, who dutifully held it down on the ground to gather the last little pile of debris she had gathered. Sweep, sweep. *"May the grace of our Lord Jesus Christ…(sweep, sweep)… the love of God (sweep, sweep)…and the sweet communion of the Holy Spirit be with you all"*

Was there no reverence? Or was it exactly the reminder we needed on this last Sunday in November?

*"Moses was keeping the flock of his father-in-law Jethro,
the priest of Midian; he led his flock beyond the wilderness,
and came to Horeb, the mountain of God.
There the angel of the Lord appeared to him
in a flame of fire out of a bush...."*

Genesis 3:1-2

Anyone who has tried to discern a call from God cannot but help be a bit envious of the burning bush put in Moses' path. Moses left the house that morning on a sheep-herding career track. He returned home committed to lead God's people out of captivity.

Somewhere in between, God appeared to Moses in a way so clear, so vivid, so real, that there was no doubt what God expected of him.

We moderns in search of God's direction are plagued with doubts. What if God sent me the sign and I misinterpreted it? What if the sign was there and I missed it all together? What if what I thought was a divine sign was just my own imagination? Was I just caught up in some euphoria of a great faith experience? Am I to base my life on whisper? What if I was wrong? We revisit that crucial moment, hoping to uncover some hidden truth that we may have missed the first time.

The story of Moses' call is depicted in a mosaic, high atop the domed ceiling of Ravenna's Basilica di San Vitale. The church, which dates back to 547AD is described in one guidebook for its "somber exterior" which "hides a dazzling internal feast of colour." Pieces of gold, white, blue, orange, red, green and yellow Murano glass (of nearby Venetian-glass fame), have been meticulously set to portray scenes from the Old Testament. In one corner Abraham holds a dagger high over Isaac's head. In another, Abel and Melchizedek offer sacrifices at the altar. And off to the side are two scenes from that fateful day in Moses' life.

Below, he tends to the sheep. Above, he is untying his sandals. However, instead of a single burning bush there is a whole brushfire of burning bushes. Tiny orange and red tiles of glass appear above little tufts of brownish-green wilderness. In total, some 27 burning bushes surround the startled shepherd. As if the heavenly message were not thorough enough, a hand pokes out of a cloud, pointing at the divine show of pyrotechnics below.

When I was trying to discern God's call to the ordained ministry, some of the most-helpful advice I received eased my intense scrutiny of one bush. "God works in infinitely-imaginative ways" said one pastor; "if it's a call from God, the signs will be abundant and creative." "Look for a pattern," said another wise soul, "have multiple signs pointed you in the same direction?" Still another person suggested I rotate the lens of discernment from zoom to wide-angle: "Look back over the past year or year and a half," she suggested, "Did the sense come to you just once? Or has it kept coming back to you? If God is truly calling you, God will keep trying to get your attention."

Apparently, even sixth-century mosaic artists knew something about putting many coloured pieces together to get a larger picture. One bright tile might be pleasurable to the sight, but does not a *feast of colour* make. One burning bush, for that matter, may catch the eye, but not like a whole forest fire.

"I am the vine and you are the branches.
Those who abide in me and I in them bear much fruit,
because apart from me you can do nothing."

John 15:5

Rushed out the door this morning. No devotion time. Quick breakfast. We grabbed lunches, city transport passes, homework, and ran to the tram stop.

One of the trams that arrives at this particular stop runs on electric current. Two long metal poles jut out from its roof, leaning back at a 45 degree angle. At their ends, two glorified coat-hangers engage with cables that are suspended over the main streets from lamp posts. The tram's free range is limited to the radius of the swivelling metal arms that grip the cables above it. Drivers need to know to stick to the prescribed path or they risk losing contact with their source of power.

As it approached our stop, we could see that the tram was packed with commuters. Suddenly, the tram veered slightly to the right to avoid an on-coming car. The tram came to a complete stop, still some distance from curbside. The startled passengers inside looked up towards the driver to see what had happened. They began pressing the buttons inside to open the doors and get out, but to no avail. *"Le porte!* C'mon, open the doors!" No movement.

A heavy-set driver got out of the tram and walked towards the back. He glanced up at the roof of his vehicle as he slipped his hands into some dirty leather work gloves. His sudden turn had jarred the two hooks from the overhead cables. The usually-upright arms sagged, one to the left side, the other to the right, like the crestfallen ears of some robotic creature. No juice.

With a flick of his wrists, he hoisted one hook, then the other, back up to the power cables. As he attached the second hook to its rightful place, the bus' turn signals resumed their blinking and the doors suddenly opened. Some people got off, cursing the delay, and rushed to the stairs of the nearby subway stop.

I guess the driver got back in and turned the ignition back on. I'm not sure, though. I had to run.

"…et in hora mortis nostrae."
(…and at the hour of our death.)

from the Ave Maria prayer

"Un caffe macchiato, un espresso!" shouted the exasperated bartender in the large cafeteria. Two men, both wearing RAI television news jackets, raised their hands, *"Qui!"* They sidled their way to the bar in between two women dressed in hospital gowns. One of the women slid her portable intravenous tube to the side to let them pass.

At a table nearby, some elderly Eastern Europeans chatted with a nun, clad in white. Salami in well-travelled wax paper was served beside a thermos of coffee.

Several *carabinieri* stood casually near the main entrance. The cordons they had tied a few hours earlier for a visiting delegation of Indian bishops were still draped along the corridor. Excitement now over, one talked on a cell phone while three of his colleagues argued over the proper directions to give to a family visiting a patient.

Across from the entrance, other police guarded a part of the lobby that had become a press room. Within the ropes, two women spoke in halting English. Fifteen or so journalists tapped keys on laptops. One man struggled with two folding chairs, attempting to arrange them in a configuration most suitable for a nap. A bouquet of international microphones fastened to a stand on the vacant dais awaited the next briefing.

Down the hall two priests conversed outside a small chapel. A photo of a much younger Pope John Paul II had been taped to the door. Inside, except for a stray set of rosaries, the pews were empty. The only noise, a steady pounding of rain on the roof.

On the hill overlooking the hospital, the downpour was soaking a herd of television trucks. A cluster of reporters smoked cigarettes under a dripping canopy of one of the campers. As if on sentry duty, 25 cameras, draped in tarps, stood on a makeshift platform, all aimed at the windows of the suite on the tenth floor. No likelihood of any papal blessing tonight. "Toothpaste!" one man called as he ran towards a parked *vespa*, "…and what else – some more *Nastro Azzurro* [beer] and a newspaper?"

One tracheotomy has brought together priests and scribes in this extended vigil. Candles light one room and spotlights another. Well outside the city gates, miles away from the Vatican, this hilltop house of cure has welcomed this strange assembly of the faithful and the frenetic, novitiates and news anchors. In the overlapping rhythms of vespers and deadlines, prayer time and air time coexist. Uncommon companions, now unified in the powerlessness of waiting, sit at the counter and pass the sugar.

*"Humour is a kind of court jester in the castle of our souls,
by which we are protected from too solemn a view
of our own importance."*

James Simpson (7)

When thousands of grieving Catholics crowded into Rome's Piazza San Pietro to mourn the death of Pope John Paul II, some held aloft banners which read, *Santo subito* (Saint immediately). These were appeals from the masses to bypass the lengthy process the Roman Catholic Church usually requires to making anyone a saint. A year or so later, when Italo-American singer Madonna brought her show to the Eternal City, one over-zealous fan carried an adapted (and feminized) version of the sign: *Santa subito*.

During the conclave in which a college of cardinals elects a new pope, the faithful gather outside Saint Peters Basilica. They wait for the white smoke to appear over the Vatican, when the suspense is partially resolved. The official announcement comes when one of the cardinals appears on a balcony and announces in Latin, according to centuries old tradition, "Habemus Papam!" ("We have a Pope!"). Not long after the election of the current pope, a well-known canned tomato sauce company came out with a new slogan: 'Habemus Sugo' ('We have a sauce').

Being that Popes John Paul II and Benedict XVI were friends, there are some popular photos of the two men together. In some store windows, their individual portraits are hung in the window, side by side. In one café, two such pictures adorn the mantle behind the bar, in between bottles of *Jagermeister* and *Grappa Julia*. On closer inspection, however, the photo on the right is of the bartender dressed for a costume party – complete with white cap, flowing robes and gold cross.

One person's sacrilege is another's satire; one's poke, another's playfulness. Is nothing sacred? Or is there something sacredly funny when the lofty are brought low? The court clown always seemed to know just when to genuflect and when to jest.

"Remember those in prison ..."

Hebrews 13:3

Across the prison courtyard, the only visible signs of humanity were the twelve or so hands through the bars of the window. Two of them clutched a small mirror, irregular in shape. Every so often, the setting sunlight would catch the little piece of glass and send a quick flash into the hall in which we were gathered.

Our choir had submitted their documents months before to sing today at San Vittore. Security had been tightened with overcrowding now at record levels: 1424 people, sometimes crammed ten-to-a-room designed to hold six. Of that total, 75 percent are estimated to be foreigners, some in prison for violent crimes, but most for missing documents, petty theft, and nowhere else to put them. One hundred of the prisoners are women. Today we were in the women's section, guests at the prison chaplain's weekly prayer in their chapel. The long dark hall had benches on either side, a simple altar at the front, and four barred windows... with that persistent flash of light entering repeatedly.

"We're happy that some of you on the outside could be with some of us on the inside," the chaplain began. The women all clapped. A thin shaft of light zig-zagged across the side wall. "What's with the light from that mirror?" I whispered to one of the regular visitors. "Oh" she said, "he's sending a message to someone. In probably in some kind of code, lines, flashes, circles, but it's a message all right."

The choir stood to sing *Immensa Grazia* (Amazing Grace). Through the open window, the sound of a Muslim muezzin calling prayer wafted across the courtyard. One of the women turned to us and smiled, as if to say, "It's OK. It's their prayer time, too." Then our choir sang an anthem which one member had written about the creation story in Genesis. As if on cue with the first day of creation, there was light through the window, dancing above the crucifix.

When it came time for the intercessory prayer, the designated person from our group stood up to read, clutching a typed page. The chaplain smiled and motioned him back to his seat. "Our sisters on the inside have prepared the prayer today for you visitors from the outside," he said, "it's in a few languages." One by one, the women stood up, saying words first in Italian, then in Romanian, then Mandarin, Arabic, Portuguese, Spanish, Russian, French... it continued for some minutes. The page of pre-planned intercessions were folded up and placed on the bench.

A woman rose to give a testimony: "I never thought I'd be in here. My four-year-old is on the outside, and I am here. But I have not lost my faith. These sisters here, and the priests, they do not judge me." Then a man, accompanied by a guard, gave his witness: "I am just one man but I have decided to represent all the other men in those other blocks," he said. "Pray for me, but pray for them, too."

The light bounced in the space between the first and second stations of the cross: one frame showing him receiving his sentence from Pilate, the next of the cross being laid on his back. The flashes, lines and circles were becoming more constant. The message was gradually getting clearer.

*"It is within... a prayerful silence that a bonding
draws us closer together"*

Roger J. Vanden Busch (8)

Ave Maria, piena di grazia, il Signore è con te. In Catholic circles like the one I'm in today, the beginning of the Hail Mary is the signal for me to bow my head and close my eyes. I don't pray the words. They are not my words. This is not my prayer.

I've been with this particular group of Catholics long enough that they understand my silence. They have since admitted to me that at first, they wondered if I was an agnostic or even an atheist. Why else would I not pray the prayer? For what other possible reason would I not make the sign of the cross when I name the Trinity?

Tu sei benedetta fra le donne e benedetto è il frutto del tuo seno, Gesù.

My silence is my respect for their tradition and a chance to pray my own prayer. But as the repetition continues, it is hard not to feel a bit lonely. They know the words. I don't. They believe in one thing; I, another. We can talk about politics, joke about foods, share stories from our childhood, but for those moments of prayer, we are different and separate.

Santa Maria, madre di Dio, prega per noi peccatori, adesso e nell'ora della nostra morte.

Today's Angelus seems to go on extra long. Somewhere in the third or fourth repetition, I am aware of Elio's burly presence moving a bit closer. He is praying, too, but his volume seems to be getting softer. Then suddenly, without explanation, he stops praying all together. His shoulder touches mine and he just stands there.

Amen.

"And be thankful."

Colossians 3:15

The Bible study theme was about thankfulness. The North American author of the curriculum we were using recalled the time when an ice storm knocked out the power supply to his town. He remarked how he had not been fully appreciative of the electricity in his home until he was without it. He compared the thankfulness of a person who had once been caught in addiction to the person who had worshipped routinely all his life. Only the one who has known real darkness fully thanks God for the light.

One woman smiled. "It is much different for us. In my village in the Philippines, we did not have power until just last year. It is hard for people here in Italy to imagine that. Here in Europe, you are always with electricity. Here in Milano, there is always light. The streets are always bright, even at one o'clock in the morning."

A man from Ghana commented, "When I lived in the village, I had a kerosene lantern, and I would carry it with me. When the sun went down it was dark, so dark, no lights at all. Just my lantern. It was enough to see my book or to find a station for news on my little battery radio."

Another Filipino woman said, "When I was young our family only had candles and they gave only a little light. The room was not so bright as this one here, but with the candle it was enough light. I will tell you something; maybe you think it is strange. Now I have been in Italy a few years. I sometimes feel a little bad that I am in a place with so much light (only minutes earlier, upon entering our classroom, she had opened the window shades turned off the electric overhead light). Do you know what I still do? You will all laugh, but when I come home from my work to my little apartment, I light a candle. I could turn on the lights, but I don't. I want to remember how little I once had. I do not want to start thinking like a rich person, who has so much and doesn't even think about how much she has. So I light that candle. Not because I have to. But because… well, maybe it is because I have to."

"Why are you cast down, O my soul?"

Psalm 42:5

After the Carnevale frolic,
most confetti rests,
pressed in crevasses
of pavement and stone,
stomped underfoot
in the plod through Lent.
But not hers.
The princess pauses
over the metal duct
which spews air
from the subways below.
With grips full of colour,
she smiles and releases.
The *coriandoli*
dance and whirl,
upward like flames,
holy incense
wafting to heaven.
A pirate observes –
sidearm poised,
his clenched fists,
filled with glitter.
A flick of his wrist
would bury his treasures;
but an opening of palm
could cast them upwards,
as if in intercession.

Together, at the Table

"Agape (Love), the early Christian love feast..."

Encyclopedia Britannica, 1911

While visiting Methodist churches in the United States this summer, we learned a thing or two about 'pot-luck dinners'. Over fried chicken and jello salad in a church in Ohio one night, someone told us that the 'pot' part referred to the dish *you* prepare; the 'luck' part is hoping that *someone else* will bring something you'll like. In some parts of Indiana, they're called 'Pitch-ins'. Someone in Michigan told us that there's a native American word that sounds like 'pat-lach' which means 'sharing'. In some European Methodist churches, we've heard them called 'Bring and Share'. The Italian Protestants describe a meal in which everyone brings something made by their own hands as an *'Agape'*.

*Agape*s as we know them at the Chiesa Metodista in Milano are eclectic. Back when this congregation was made up of only Italians, we're told that the meal consisted of a *primo, secondo, insalata, dolce* and *caffe* – courses in a traditional Italian meal. Now the table has changed; it reflects all the different cultures present in the congregation: cous-cous from Sierra Leone, fried plantains from Ghana, Tandoori chicken from India, pansit soy noodles from the Philippines, and of course, some kind of pasta. Familiar dishes look like old friends. Other dishes may elicit (as sometimes happens in our family) a sceptical raised eyebrow or crinkled nose. When all are served onto one paper plate, an interesting encounter occurs. Recipes from two or three different continents meet, spices from two different racks find their way onto the same dish. Tastes blend. Spaghetti Bolognese takes on a hint of curry.

For the culinary purist, such a mixture would be a fiasco. In the church, it is a sign of creating space for the other, even the one who is *very* other. To paraphrase (loosely) Luke 6:32, *'If we love only those foods which are the same as ours, what does that say of us?'*. Part of agape is sliding our own casserole over to make a place for someone else's dish. *"Mangia! Mangia!"* ("Eat! Eat!") is one side of hospitality. The other may be: "Let me try one of those orange things. What do you call them again?"

At one of those American church visits, a woman approached us: "Do you know that our United Methodist Women's group has as its theme this year, 'Who's at the Table?'. We're looking at the groups of people that the church has excluded from the table over the years: African-Americans, Native Americans. Actually, it's been kind of painful to think about. But it has made me look differently at the table – about who we welcome, and who we *need* to welcome. Maybe we should think of the table in the fellowship hall as part of the Lord's Table."

Agape, indeed.

"Signore, vieni a noi e sediti alla nostra mensa..."
("Lord, come among us and sit at our table...")

From an Italian table prayer

The city's Teatro Manzoni is presenting a revival of William Arthur Rose's play, 'Guess Who's Coming to Dinner?'. In this version, the roles immortalized by Katherine Hepburn and Spencer Tracy are played by Gianfranco D'Angelo and Ivana Monti. Instead of 1967 affluent San Francisco, 'Indovina Chi Viene a Cena?' is set in modern day Milano. And in a decidedly African twist, Sidney Poitier's Dr. John Wade Prentice is played by an actor named Fatimata Dembele. Four decades since the controversial film brought one couple and their two American families – one white and one black – into contact with one another around a dinner table, the play has been reworked and readapted for an Italian audience.

Perhaps that is the reason why, four decades after a film showed an Anglo-American girl shocking her parents by bringing home her African-American boyfriend, the same play is resonating with Italian theatre-goers. The guest could have any number of nationalities. Even in a multicultural metropolis such as Milano, mealtime companionship is, for the most part, homogeneous. Lunch-hour café tables seldom reflect the statistical diversity of the city.

Even though worship at our church brings together many cultures, most of us return to eat the rest of the week's meals with people who look like us. Family supper time remains sadly segregated. On any given evening, Italian pasta is served in one home, Filipino pansit in another, Ghanaian fried plantains in another, and Indian curried fish in another. The ingredients have been purchased at different stores. They have been cooked in different kitchens, by recipes written in different languages. The only time these varied dishes are placed on the same table is after church in the fellowship hall. They, and the people who prepare them, live in largely separate, parallel worlds. Parallel lives, like parallel lines, do not meet.

Which makes church pot-luck suppers here even more significant. If only once a week, the D'Angelos and the Dembeles sit down for a meal together. A slice offered here, a glass refilled there. A polite conversation at one end of the table, introductions at another, shared laughter at another. And lives that never looked to intersect, now bend and meet. Be it the altar or the folding table, someone else at the table gives encounters like those potential and promise. Look who came to dinner...

> *"The bread that we break, is it not a sharing*
> *in the body of Christ?"*

I Corinthians 10:16

The faithful formed a circle around the altar. My colleague removed the cloth from the bread and the cup.

Christ our Lord invites to his table all who love him...

I was vaguely aware of something moving in front of us. We continued through the liturgy, into The Great Thanksgiving.

It is right, and a good and joyful thing, always and everywhere to give thanks to you, Father Almighty...

Yes, it *was* something moving. It was a hand waving. I glanced up. The hand's owner, a 14-year-old boy, smiled at me, as if satisfied to have finally caught my attention. With one hand he held up two fingers. With the other, he shielded the sign, as if to hide from others this secret exchange going on between us. Not sure whether to receive his gesture as a sign of spontaneous friendliness or a protest against the war, I continued.

And so with all your people on earth and all the company of heaven...

More waving.

Holy, holy, holy Lord, God of power and might, heaven and earth are full of your glory. Hosanna in the highest. Blessed is he who comes in the name of the Lord. Hosanna in the highest.

As my colleague and I lifted the chalice and patin, and the stewards came forward to prepare to serve, the young man approached us. "Pssst. Pastors. Could I take two pieces of bread today? One for my mother? She has to work this morning." We both nodded to him.

As we moved around the circle in his direction, I noticed that he was digging in his pockets for something. He retrieved a little plastic bag, the kind that holds pocket tissues.

The body of Christ, given for you.

He reached out his hand and received a piece of bread. Then he reached out and took another.

The blood of Christ, shed for you.

He dipped one piece in the chalice, then put it in his mouth. Then he touched the other piece of bread to the wine, carefully put it in the bag, and tucked it into his jeans pocket.

This afternoon, the sacrament – slightly pressed – will go by subway to the train station. It will ride the train for another half-hour, then be taken on foot the mile or so to a one-room apartment.

And tonight, after the day-shift gets out, at a small kitchen table, a weary soul will lower herself into a chair. A young celebrant will take out little plastic bag. And a holy and living sacrifice will be shared.

"…the members of the body that seem to be weaker
are indispensable…"

I Corinthians 12:22

In the Methodist church north of Milano, the mother of the eight-year-old boy whom I was sitting next to, gave him a pointed glare across the sanctuary. Even though they were a family from Cote d'Ivoire, she was communicating in an international form of parent-language that I understood well: the intense (but silent), disapproving (but hopefully too subtle to be public), corrective (but ever so polite – after all this is church) shake of the head. Message received, he sat back down. He had bravely made it through a long sermon (mine), seemingly endless intercessions, and now was biding his time through the announcements. Looking for something else to occupy himself, he picked up the order of worship. With his finger, he tapped his way down it, as if mentally checking off the things we had already accomplished. His finger stopped at the upcoming Holy Communion. His sigh of impatience was audible. Another glare from his mother shot across the sanctuary.

She, like many foreigners, may well have been feeling the social pressure that many in these churches know well: behaviour must not only be adequate, but stellar, so as not to reflect badly on an entire family or cultural group. In order to enter gracefully into a congregation in which your colour, your nationality, your traditions are different; misbehaviour risks confirming stereotypes and being excluded.

A grey-haired *nonna* (grandmother), sitting in front of us, seemed more aware of the exchanges going on than I had realized. She turned around and gave the boy a pat on his head. Then, just as conspicuously, she turned and looked at his parents across the way and smiled reassuringly. Perhaps she was oblivious to the jingling of offering money in his cupped hands, or perhaps just feigning deafness.

When it came time for the distribution of the elements, our little friend became even more restless. The congregation gathered in a circle around the altar. The boy remained in his seat, absorbed in his hymnal-stacking experiment, while everyone was busy pushing back pews and reaching for one another's hands. The *nonna* let go of her husband's hand and walked over to the boy. "Come on," she said, in sing-song rhyme, "you little *chiacchierone*…you little *catenone*" (meaning 'chatterbox' and 'little link in the chain'). "Come over here. Take my hand. Stand between us."

"...we are surrounded by so great a cloud of witnesses..."

Hebrews 12:1

After a church gathering on the first Sunday of November, I found myself next to two of the older men of the congregation. Riccardo is old enough to be my father; Giorgio could be my grandfather. With nimble hospitality, they drew me into their conversation as if casually setting another place for me at the family dinner table. "Did you know," said the older Giorgio, "that Riccardo's father, may he rest in peace, and I were dear friends?" He wrapped his frail arm around Riccardo's shoulders. Riccardo smiled and nodded, "Yes, you and Dad were very close."

Like walking me through the family attic and pausing at each framed photo or dusty trophy, they told me stories... stories both personal and political, which traced their way through the reigns of kings and dictators, church persecutions and congregational mergers; tales remote in time and locale, but close enough to moisten the eyes of the storytellers.

"You recall," Giorgio said, "how your father and I would always take communion together? Do you remember seeing us do that, Riccardo?" Riccardo wrinkled his nose, as if conjuring up the image. "Every time there would be the Holy Supper in the church, we would look for each other. He might be sitting with his family on one side of the sanctuary, and I, with mine, on the other. No matter where we were seated at the time, we would find each other, and then we would meet at a certain place near the altar. And every time, when the pastor served us, we would be standing together."

Riccardo smiled.

"And you remember your father;" Giorgio continued with a mischievous tilt to his head, "he and I did not always agree on our politics. You know what he believed, and he believed it strongly. You know my views – I still have them – and were he still alive, I would still be telling him how wrong he was. But when it came time for communion, we always stood together, side by side."

As I stood with my elders, I understood a bit better how these two men could find enough space in their own hearts to open this community to foreign immigrants 20 years ago. They did not invent kindness and mercy. Those things were created by a force long before them. The same spirit of kindness and mercy that could make their forefathers overlook the lesser differences between them, is now at work in them. They are the ones who now stand shoulder to shoulder at Holy Communion with persons of vastly different backgrounds and cultures and opinions.

Even if we were in an Italian Protestant church that doesn't believe in saints, it felt like All Saints' Day. Black and white photos take on colour. Inked names on yellowed pages in the church register are given voices and habits and beliefs.

*"In the same way, he took the cup also, after supper,
saying, 'This cup is the new covenant in my blood.
Do this, as often as you drink it, in remembrance of me'."*

I Corinthians 11:25

One tram and one subway ride from our church is the Chiesa della Santa Maria delle Grazie, the home of Leonardo da Vinci's, *The Last Supper*. Painted some 500 years ago, the artist offered his vision of the Holy Thursday meal. Leonardo's use of lines and angles draws onlookers into the scene. Recently restored colours make the disciples' faces, the glasses on the table and the bread on the plates seem almost real.

That is, however, if you are able to get inside the building. Reservations must be made weeks or months in advance. Each day busloads of Japanese and American tourists, cameras and guidebooks in hand, disembark in the nearby piazza. Pilgrims, art history majors, and aficionados of *The Da Vinci Code* wait outside for hours, hoping that an eight-Euro ticket may suddenly become available. Every 15 minutes, 25 ticket holders are admitted into a small waiting room. After guards inspect tickets, purses and pockets, the group is herded through sliding plexiglass doors into another holding area. At the stroke of the quarter-hour, automatic doors open into the darkened refectory, where the famous fresco awaits. Fifteen minutes later, the group is escorted to the gift shop.

Across town at the Chiesa Metodista, access to the Lord's Supper is a bit easier. The Italian seminary student stretches her arms wide to invite the faithful to the table. Persons from Europe, Africa, Asia, North and South America make their way up the aisles. Some who need gestures to understand one another smile and make space for each other. French and American children wiggle in between adults and hold out their cupped hands. Two Filipino girls play on the violin 'Let us break bread together'. Indian women cover their heads with colourful scarves as they approach the table. Ghanaian men gently place their tambourines on their chairs as they walk to the front. Latecomers, straight off the night-shift, make their way into the circle. Someone hastily brings more bread from the side to ensure that everyone will eat. Another refills the chalice with a large jug of homemade red wine.

Of this community, some are white collar and others wear no collar. Some clean offices and others run offices. Some hire live-in help, others are live-in help. Some search for housing, others find a place for the stranger. Some feel like hosts, others like guests. Some will join their relatives for dinner afterwards, and some will use an international phone card to call loved ones far away. Some come here by subway and others drive from the suburbs. Some have known discrimination based on denomination, others have known persecution for their faith. Believers of disparate languages, experience, temperaments, outlooks and opinions stand shoulder to shoulder, heads bowed.

No barriers to this table. Observers are drawn in. Onlookers become participants. This is our vision of the Holy Thursday meal.

Together, following Jesus

Chic bar
wall-mirror
shaped like a cross,
a jagged mosaic
of glass tiles.
Add some lipstick,
check your hair,
does this colour suit me?
How do I look?
Reflection is distorted, fragmented, disconnected, detached imperfect;
eyes crossed, one ear too low, oversize mouth, nose off-centre, eyebrows
not aligned.
Head disembodied
from heart and gut.
An assembly
of pieces,
this image.
Lacks smoothness
or beauty
or integration.
A mess.
Apart.
Step back, though,
Stop looking
in the mirror
dimly.
View the shape
given you
in its outline
and form.
From here,
in this light,
you look...
stunning.

"...imitate what is good"

3 John 1:11

When the artist Michelangelo died on 18 February 1564, an unfinished stone carving was found among his belongings. The stone statue, a depiction of Mary holding the lifeless figure of Jesus, was called the *Rondanini Pieta*, and it now resides in Milano. It lacks the polished beauty, the awe-inspiring realism, the attention to detail that is evident in the artist's most famous statue of David. The face of Christ is, in some places, rough and vague. The figure of Mary is shrouded in a cloth. The two figures merge at the shoulder, their individual definition revealed in some places, hidden in others. On the right side of Jesus, detached from his body, but part of the overall block of stone is a masterfully crafted arm. The arm is in proportion to the rest of Christ's body and is positioned in a way that fits with the rest of his body... if, that is, it were attached, which, for some reason, it is not.

What purpose did that arm serve? Art experts have argued over the answer. When some of Michelangelo's sketches were later discovered, a detailed drawing of that arm suggested that it had received particular attention from the artist. Based on that sketch, scholars surmise that Michelangelo was using it as a *punto di riferimento* (a point of reference) for the second statue. Namely, as he worked on the unfinished part of Jesus' body, he needed to have an already finished part as a guide.

In other words, to imagine Jesus clearly, he needed a model. Creating an image of Jesus required not only bursts of creative energy, but careful precision, almost as if the artist was admitting to himself that he could not conjure up an entire image of Jesus in his head. He needed a point of reference, some accurate depiction, some almost-human likeness to help him create a recognizable likeness of Christ. A careful viewing to his left, a move with his chisel on the right. A frequent study on one side gave birth to a new creation on the other. And slowly, measured by each particle of dust collecting below, a new image of the original Jesus was being shaped.

Together, as the Body of Christ

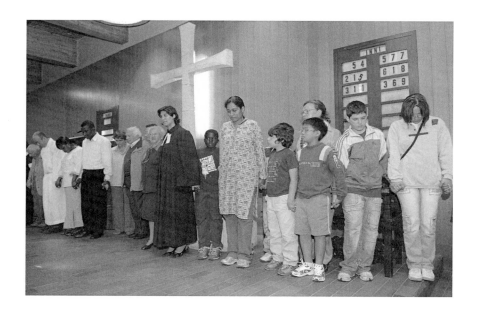

"But let there be spaces in your togetherness
and let the winds of the heavens dance between you.
Love one another but make not a bond of love:
let it be rather a moving sea between the shores of your souls."

Kahlil Gibran (1)

The church flooded again last night (the Italian word is *allagato*, which might be translated as *laked*). Because it happens so often, we've developed a certain post-deluvian routine. The unofficial bailing team phone chain is activated. Members arrive, grab a bucket and a mop, and jump into action. The conversation among the team of bailers usually drifts from exasperation, to questioning Leonardo da Vinci's underground river scheme, and eventually to wondering where the other helpers are. In the frustration and tedium caused by the calamity, the resentment bubbles up to the surface. And we look for somewhere (or someone) where it can be dumped. There's an Italian saying '*Non sappiamo a che santo di grapparsi*', which means, 'We don't know which saint to complain to'. Often, the accusations are charged along pre-existing biases: "Where is the building administrator?" or "Why don't the city planners do anything?" or "Where are the …? Why isn't … here helping?" (when blame is sometimes thrown indiscriminately at particular cultural groups represented in the church).

The conventional wisdom about intercultural congregations seems to be that if we are truly a unified congregation, we will all pitch in. Which is, of course, the truth. But this dream of unity is often a bit airbrushed: smiling people, side by side, assembled in a bucket brigade – a South Korean hands off to an Italian, who in turn, passes the bucket to an Indonesian, who happily dumps it into the drain. *'I'd like to teach the world to sing in perfect harmony'* plays in the background, and when the water's all bailed they give each other high fives.

But today's clean-up efforts didn't look like that at all. Several Indians, who got off work at 8:00pm that evening, came to help for a few hours after work. The next morning, several retired Italians came to bail. In the afternoon, a couple of students came after school. Each squad spoke in their own tongue. There was laughter and jokes, but no translation necessary. While the groups didn't even see one other to hand off the mops, there was a unity to the goal.

One of our pastoral roles that has unfolded is to inform each group of who'd been there last. "Well, the water's a couple of inches lower this morning thanks to the group that was here last night."

A colleague in another intercultural congregation once commented that he discovered, over time, that unity looks more like loose interconnection. Much is done separately, which makes the times of togetherness all the more meaningful. He called it "being inter-connected but not always together".

The Sunday school rooms are dry tonight, thanks to the efforts of many. The teams didn't meet on Monday. But on Sunday they did.

"In a true community we will not choose our companions,…"

Parker Palmer (2)

Arnold's in the house.
No, Arnold's on the house.
Actually, he's on the wall,
stencilled in green and black.
Why him?
Why here?
Sitcom idol
Gary Coleman,
frozen in time:
cherubic, ten-year-old,
dimples and smile.
No Mr. Drummond or Kimberly.
Just him:
Wha'chyou talkin' about, Willis?
I don't know.
How'd he get there?
I wasn't looking.
Maybe while we were asleep,
someone sprayed him up there.
Their standard-bearer –
our graffiti.
Their tag –
our vandalism.
Their emblem –
our intruder.
No one asked permission.
He just showed up.
Now I've got to see him,
every time I enter the sanctuary.
I don't come to church,
to look at the likes of him.
Can't relate to his character.
Didn't choose his company.
Whoever's responsible –
did they not know
that this is *my* house??

"On account of this child,
a sword will pierce your own soul, too."

Luke 2:35 (adapted)

"For unto us a child is born..." the fourth-grader read from the book of Isaiah. The sanctuary was filled with children, youths and adults for the annual Sunday school Christmas programme on this third Sunday of Advent. Children adjusted costumes, clutched sheet music and scripts.

For the youngest member of the congregation, this would be her last Sunday here. Today, amidst the donkeys and the shepherds, 'Elena' would be dedicated. Her baptism would happen two weeks later in a village church in a northern province of the Philippines. On that day, however, she will be surrounded by different members of the church family, by other faces, not yet known to her. She will be held in someone else's arms. Her parents will not be there. They will remain in Italy.

Both of Elena's parents left the poverty of their homeland to try to make a living in Europe. Mopping floors and sweeping sidewalks in Milano, they can earn four times what they might earn back home. And here, in between late shifts a few weeks before Advent, Elena was born. Hers is one face of globalization.

And so two days before a relative would accompany her to the Philippines, her parents brought her to the front of the sanctuary. The rings under their eyes showed weeks of the strains of new parenthood, and also the weight of the decision they had been wrestling with for the past nine months. Neither parent is documented. Neither, under the current laws, has sufficient income to warrant documentation. Their combined income barely puts enough food on their table. If they do find more work, they worry about how they would care for their baby. So, following the path trod by so many immigrant couples before them, they have made other arrangements.

Some members had tried to convince them to keep the child here. Others had sought to find employment for them. One family was able to give the mother three hours of work per week, but that would not be enough.

They walked to the altar and stood in front of the tempera-painted manger scene. Handing us the baby, wrapped in a white blanket, the mother sobbed, and the father inhaled in rapid, shallow breaths. The ritual held no joy, no promise of the future, no opportunity for the community to fulfill vows.

All around the congregation, we could see tears on the faces of many of the Italian members. The faces of the other immigrant families appeared solemn, but dry. One young immigrant mother had just returned from leaving her own two-month old daughter with an aunt. Another couple was only recently reunited with their six-year-old son after he was raised by his grandparents. Another couple has not seen their children in four years. They have stood here, too.

We wondered if Elena's parents would come to church on Christmas Eve. The story of the arrival of a baby, of adoring shepherds and magi, might be too much to hear. Or perhaps, in the government census, a ruler's decrees, a forced migration, and in the ominous warning to a young mother that her own soul would be pierced on account her infant, they may see enough pain in the details of *that* story to find some reassurance of Emmanuel, God with them, in their own.

"…let your light shine before others, so that they may see your good works and give glory to your Father in heaven."

Matthew 5:16

He was describing an ecumenical round-table discussion of the previous night. "They set up the rostrum in the cathedral. Everyone was there," he said, "They had this big long table up on the dais. All the guests sat on chairs behind the table. In front of each of us were little name tags. But you got the feeling that some guests were more equal than others. I mean, everyone was courteous to me, but it felt like they didn't really want to hear anything I had to say. I felt like I was… as if…. like I was *prezzemolo*."

Leave it to an Italian to describe a situation with just the right culinary image. *Prezzemolo* is parsley. A condiment. A dressing. Parsley is certainly not a main course, except perhaps, for rabbits. It is on the side. It has a bit of taste to it, but not one that has diners kissing their fingers with delight, as in: "That parsley tonight – did you taste it? It was absolutely out of this world!". Parsley adds a bit of colour, but it does not draw attention to itself. It merely makes the other dishes look more appetizing. It is often ignored, left on the plate while attention is paid to the other, more attractive choices.

Who has not known the experience of feeling insignificant, a window-dressing, the side-dish? I heard a sermon years ago preached by an African-American pastor, in which she recounted sitting on a rostrum with a group of white, male preachers. "After a while," she said, "I began to feel that I was there merely to represent only one or two of my particular characteristics. I was not there to be fully me." She told the story as a way to exhort her listeners to 'get off the rostrum'.

"There is nothing enlightened about shrinking so that other people won't feel insecure around you," Nelson Mandela said in his 1994 presidential inauguration speech. "We were born to make manifest the glory of God within us. It is not just in some of us; it's in everyone. And as we let our light shine, we unconsciously give other people permission to do the same…"

In another inaugural address, a preacher from Nazareth spoke to people accustomed to being ignored, not fully valued, to shrinking. In God's eyes, he said, you are not invisible or insignificant. You, he said, are salt. You, he said, are a city on a hill. You, he said, are light. No *prezzemolo*.

"If the whole body were an eye, where would the hearing be?"

Corinthians 12:17

Display in the optician's window,
full of noses –
plastic mounts prepared for glasses;
but for now,
just an assembly of shnozzes,
inhabiting the same bit of shelf.
Short ones, broad ones, pointy ones –
a certain variety,
but within limits;
a life together,
but disconnected.
All in all,
a manageable diversity.
Easier that way, no?
Gets cumbersome,
the whole body thing.
Operating in different locales,
the nose and the toes
could be excused for rarely meeting;
related but distant:
second cartilage, twice-removed,
remains an unknown soul,
remote and unattached,
understood only in part,
viewed only in shadow,
from contorted angles.
So different, these parts;
could be excused
for isolating
in their own regions.

Shelf-noses
could sniffle together
about spectacles, sinuses, sneezes –
withdraw into the comfort
of their common experience.
That all this
flesh and bone
can sometimes act in sync,
suggests that maybe,
just maybe,
You really did
arrange the members of the body
as you chose.

"So the last will be first…"

Matthew 20:16

As we were walking along via Tamburini, my friend grabbed my arm. "Do you see this sign?" He pointed to a marble plaque on the brick wall beside us.

Here lived Giuseppina Pizzigoni (1870-1947) … The founder the Scuola Rinnovata di Milano.

"Have you ever heard of her? Do you know what the *Scuola Rinnovata* was?"

I shook my head.

"I learned about her when I was in school. She was a teacher in a suburb, a not very nice suburb outside Milano. She was teaching like the other teachers, but then she thought things needed to be different."

"Until that time, in schools, the slow students always went to the back of the class. If you could not answer a question, you went to the back seat. Only the good students could come to the front desks. If you were ignorant, you would stay ignorant."

"Giuseppina Pizzigoni said, 'No, this is not the right way to do it.' She said that the weakest students should not go to the back of the classroom. It would always keep them down, under the others this way. Instead, she said, we should try to make every student intelligent. Not just help the smart ones, not just say to the smart ones, 'You did very well!' Not just say to the ignorant ones, 'You did very bad!' Teachers should try to make everyone smart. No front chairs. No back chairs."

"Like Jesus, no? He was like a teacher. He did not want to leave people in the back all the time. He wanted to bring everybody to the front, right?"

"Many people are good at talking about what they are doing, but in fact do little. Others do a lot but don't talk about it. They are the ones who make and sustain community."

Jean Vanier (3)

The geriatrics of the city's public transportation fleet would have to be the trams. These faded box cars of metal have rattled down their tracks for nearly 90 years. Their wooden panel interior and frosted lamp shades recall a bygone era. As one Milanese journalist has noted, the only change to them since the 1920s is a recent coat of orange paint.

They move with the grace of an elderly rhinoceros; our fourth floor apartment jiggles when they rumble past our building. Every so often they will carelessly clip a rear-view mirror off an unfortunately parked car. Pedestrians seem to know not to risk a hasty crossing in front of a tram, because trying to stop one is akin to slamming on the breaks of the QE II in the middle of the Atlantic.

When it comes to respect on the byways of the city, these old codgers rank pretty low. On the street intimidation index, there is no contest between them and the sleek Ferraris, Bartolini delivery vans, and aggressive taxis. Two-wheeled *vespas* whiz around them like bees.

The poor tram driver sits, wedged into a tiny triangular cubby hole at the front of the vehicle. Perched on a little stool, he (they are usually men) peers up at truck drivers and passenger buses. The clunky knobs and levers above his knees appear to have been scavenged off Model-T Fords. No matter what kind of horse-power brought him to the tram depot this morning, he has had to forfeit a bit of his masculinity to sit at the controls of the vehicular equivalent to a donkey. On a clear stretch with no traffic lights or stop signs, he just might be able to keep pace with the grandmothers pedalling their bikes home from the market.

There is no place in which the tram looks more ancient or more impotent than at a busy intersection. Always a flurry of illegal passes, run red lights, exceeded speed limits, and only a casual recognition of lanes; the tram frequently gets trapped in the middle. The logjam is often accompanied by a cacophony of horns. Buses trumpet, ambulances wail, vespas honk, and the tram, with all its might… lets out a gentle ring, the sound a child's tricycle bell might make if it had a potholder on top of it. No one seems to notice. In a noise competition, the quiet tram would not even win a bronze medal. In all the sound and fury, its voice is too meek.

Yet whenever city planners threaten to send them to the scrap heap and rely more on subway and bus transportation, people protest. Commuters continue to depend on them to get to places. Parents prefer to see their children off to school on a tram rather than entrust them to the bowels of the metro. Without flash or dazzle, these mute servants do their work. And a city that shows little outward appreciation for them, must begrudgingly admit that our community would be lost without them.

"Diversity is the perfection of the universe"

Thomas Aquinas (4)

The young woman stood between the two pre-teen girls. It was Thursday afternoon, and the anthem they were preparing for Sunday's worship was not coming together. "You're doing well," she said, her words echoing in the empty church sanctuary, "but you have not yet quite found the balance between your two voices."

"You each have such beautiful voices," she continued, "but they are not identical. Your voices are beautiful in different ways. Don't shy away from singing in your own voice. Don't try to sing like Beyonce or Anastasia, but like yourself. Sing with your own voice, the voice *you* were given. Harmony will come, but only when you are each singing strongly in your own voice. You'll be able to blend better when you have first found heard your own voice for itself."

The girls looked at each other and giggled.

"Don't worry about who's singing lead and who's singing harmony. This song requires two strong voices. Instead of thinking about your two parts as melody and harmony, think of yourselves with equally important parts. No melody and harmony. Just two melodies, both strong, each seeking to blend with the other melody."

One of the girls cupped her face in her hands in mock exasperation. The other tilted her head to the side, seemingly try to take in this complicated lesson.

The piano accompaniment started up again. The girls looked at each other, nodded their heads in unison and started.

"Take it again," the woman urged them. They sang it again. More coaching. And again. More direction. And another time.

At the end they glanced wearily over at their teacher. "How was that?" asked one of them sheepishly. "You two," she said with a smile, "did it *perfectly.*"

"What God has made clean, you must not call profane."

Acts 10:15

The young Italian university student was on a roll. Discussion in the working group of Waldensian, Methodists and Baptists about drafting a statement on integration was ricocheting back and forth across the room. While making a passionate speech on the subject, she paused, seemingly searching for the right word. "We need a... we need a... we need a *contaminazione mutuale* (mutual contamination) between Italians and foreigners... in our society, our schools, our churches."

Immediately, someone asked her for clarification. "Young lady, don't you think that word *contaminazione* is a little inappropriate?" he asked. "Contamination would suggest that the foreigners are dirty."

"Not only that," piped up someone else, "but for some of us who are old enough to remember, that word brings back unpleasant memories from the years of *fascismo*. In those days, the state was looking for the best Italians, the purest citizens. It had a very strict idea of who was and who wasn't considered pure Italian. There were laws to keep things so."

"Yes," added someone else. "I would use a more gentle word, like *influence*, or *impact*?"

"I'm not sure that those words are strong enough," a middle-aged woman said, coming to the student's defence. "We talk a lot about integration, and being the church together. Sometimes we talk and talk, but we don't want to get our hands dirty. We say all the right things about loving the stranger and all. But when it comes down to it, do we really want to be *changed* by them?" Arms were summarily crossed around the circle.

"For example," she continued, "do we want them to come in our churches so that we can show society how welcoming we are; but at the same time, not be willing to allow them to change our congregations? Contamination is something you try to keep from happening. You wash your hands so that you don't carry someone else's germs into your home. You get vaccinated so some disease doesn't infect you. So yes, we should use that word *contaminazione*. It reminds us not to be so safe."

Peter, after all, wasn't really converted until he ate what he had previously thought of as contaminated.

*"Father, protect them in your name that you have given me,
so that they may be one, as we are one."*

John 17:11

*"...continue in what you have learned and firmly believed,
knowing from whom you learned it..."*

Matthew 10:34-35

The word *ghetto* is actually an Italian invention. It was coined in Venice around the same time that the Protestant Reformation was happening in northern Europe. The city was reputed for its tolerant attitudes towards Jews. However, with the influx of Sephardic Jews in the early 1500s, the city leaders decided to isolate the Jewish community (rather than expel, as was being done in other European cities at the time). The only access to the ghetto in Venice were two bridges. Otherwise, it was completely isolated by canals. The Jews were required to stay inside the ghetto after midnight until dawn, and on all Christian holidays.

The word lingers and gets new uses. "I object to any kind of ghetto-isation of the church," cried one church member at a recent church council meeting. "We should be together. We are one congregation. Not everyone off doing their own thing. How is that unity?" In this sense the word is tinged with a bit of hurt: Why are your gates closed? Why are you separated from us? Are we allowed in?

He's right, of course. Ghetto walls have no place in the church. Any fulfillment of Jesus' high priestly prayer – *that they may all be one* – requires much from us. Conversations more open to include the newcomer. Committees more attentive to the person whose name no members yet know. Lunch time place settings more fluid. Language groups more dispersed. Old friends more willing to *un-clique* themselves.

And yet, during times of persecution – even behind iron gates, away from the barking of guard dogs, beyond the check points – ghettos became defiant colonies against the surrounding mayhem. Often schools, community government, and theatres all found a way to continue. Worship in the ghetto was crucial, offering a place where the holy words were taught, the sacred songs sung, the festivals observed... where the faithful stayed faithful. *When you venture outside this neighbourhood, my child, don't forget who we – here in the ghetto – have taught you to be.*

Modern ghettos can be the place to find the food your grandmother used to cook. Its boom boxes echo with music not fully appreciated several blocks away.

In the ghetto you can speak without repeating yourself. In the ghetto they know your name (your *birth* name, not the name you use to blend in with those outside the ghetto). In the ghetto you can leave your children with the neighbours. In short, in a scary world, the ghetto can feel like home.

So, is the ghetto-isation of the church all a bad thing? Perhaps not, but only if the gates are kept unlocked and the bridges to the outside are used often.

The Venetian ghetto still exists. It is home to a *yeshiva*, two active synagogues, a kosher restaurant and several Jewish shops. Yet there are pizzerias and kebab shops, too. Visitors come and go. Identity continues, only without the walls.

*"And the Ethiopian man invited Philip
to get in the chariot and sit beside him."*

Acts 8:31, adapted

The story of Philip and the Ethiopian eunuch came up in the lectionary in May this year. Their intercultural chariot encounter happened to appear the same week that the Italian government considered a proposal to reserve one car of Milano's subway for Milano-born residents only. Such is the desire on the part of some persons to keep people separate.

Recently members of our congregation have made a few trips together (although not by chariot or subway). Over Easter weekend several young people attended a youth gathering near Rome. Five nationalities were represented in the group that departed from Milano's Stazione Centrale, and many more were at the conference itself. The theme of the meeting was 'Ethics', a contentious topic that highlights strong theological differences between European, African and Asian Christians. On the train ride back to Milano, the MP3 players never seemed to make it out of the backpacks. In one compartment second-generation immigrants talked (in Italian) about feeling expectations from their parents not to become too Italian. In another compartment other foreigners argued about their role in the Italian church. "They need our prophetic voice here," said one. "No," said another, "you do not enter someone's home and criticize the host." The conversation continued for several hours.

A few weeks later our congregation sent a large delegation to a national gathering of Italian Methodists. Some went by car, others by train, and one group by camper. In the camper were five church members who had known one another from various church activities, but had never made a five-hour road trip together. Along the way they combined Italian, English, Tagalog, a little high school Spanish and a lot of sign language. The next week, one of the participant's spouses told us, "My husband couldn't stop talking about that trip! He didn't say much at all about the meetings... but he talked on and on about what he learned on the journey."

You never know what's going to happen when two people ride in a chariot together.

"People were bringing little children to him…"

Mark 10:13

"One day, when Jesus was talking to many people," she began the lesson with the children, "the disciples told the children to stay away. But Jesus did not want them to stay away. He wanted them to come close to him. And he told the people, 'Let the little children come to me, each one of them.' Do you know that the Kingdom of heaven belongs to *them?*"

"If you were there that day, where would you want to sit?" At first, the children seemed a bit distracted by the glistening green and pink sequins on her Indian sari. After a moment of silence, one, then another pointed to spots on a poster she was holding.

She turned behind her and picked up a stack of paper, cut into shapes, and held them up one by one – figures of children, in different dress, with different skin colours and facial features.

"Let's see," she said as she held up one of the cut-outs. "This one has cinnamon skin… kind of like… yours!" She handed to one of the boys. "And this one has mahogany skin… which looks a little like…. you." She held it out for a little girl to take. One by one, as if matching colour cards and skin tone, she held each figure up, then found just the right match. A kind of racial profiling done with such grace; a blunt recognition of colour differences named with such affirmation.

"Now here's a little Sellotape. Place it on the back and put your figure where you would like to be. They swarmed to the poster and fixed their images to it. When they stepped back, the picture showed nine colourful faces – tan, pink, dark chocolate, cream – clustered around the man with the olive-skin face.

*"Il nodo... nell'inconografia cristiana è spesso simbolo
di unione nella comunità."*
*(The knot... in Christian iconography is a symbol
of unity within the Christian community.)*

From an Italian art history textbook

They have been members of this congregation for over 30 years. They live in a five-bedroom apartment (with a Jacuzzi), own a car, and two motor-cycles. When the elevator in the building doesn't work, he calls the technician, who arrives within hours. She leaves for work after breakfast, arriving at her office at 8:30, shows her security card to the attendant, and parks her car in the firm's garage in time to get to the staff meeting. Her job requires her to travel to conferences in Europe, Canada and the United States. While they're at work, a maid comes to clean their house, water their plants, and walk their dog. They will go to the coast again this year, where they own a home.

They have been members of this church for 15 years. They live in a two-room apartment with their two children, and own a used car. The elevator of their building has not worked in seven months; they carry their children and groceries to the sixth floor. He gets to his job at 5:30am, mops and sweeps the office before the employees arrive, then hurries back to his car before 8:00am, when the parking fees go into effect on the street. She cleans the house of an Italian family. With their com-bined income, they are saving up to visit their homeland two years from now. For the time being, though, while they wait for their immigration documents to be renewed, they are not allowed to leave the country.

Sunday afternoon, a group of members had stayed after to sing hymns. They were largely of the same nationality. Quite unexpectedly, a new-comer of a different nationality – one of the people described above – came to the door, and asked, "Mind if I sing with you today?" A chair was unfolded and an extra copy of sheet music passed down the row. And even if for only a few stanzas, people whose worlds never meet, sat next to one another.

The knot of Christian community begins with a rope. The rope begins with several strings. Each string has its threads and each thread its tiny fibers. It is those fine and delicate strands that ultimately give strength to the *ties that bind our hearts in Christian love.*

"…otherwise, the journey will be too much for you."

I Kings 19:7

Italian cyclists take their sport seriously. Not a weekend goes by when groups in similarly-coloured uniforms don't whiz through the city, across the flatlands near Milano or in the hills to the north. Cycling clubs, cycling associations, cycling teams – it seems less a mode of individual fitness, and more a comradeship on wheels. Because they often race on Sundays, someone has called cycling the *'Italians' alternative church'*.

A friend was telling me about his having found a cycling club in his village. "I've only been going for a few weeks," he said, "so I'm really not a member of the club yet. But they treat me like a member. One of the men told me that to get more out of my pedalling, I should raise my seat by a centimeter. One of the other members disagreed: I would raise it by a centimetre and a half." Members of his new community gathered around his back wheel and discussed the matter.

"When we went out on our first ride together," my friend recounted, "I noticed that when they are riding in single file, if the lead cyclist swerves even slightly to avoid a manhole cover or something lying in the street, he'll bring one hand behind his back and make a waving motion to warn the next cyclist, who in turn does the same motion for the following person."

"As the lead rider approaches a traffic light, he looks both ways to see if there is any oncoming traffic. If the road is clear, he waves the next rider on. This helps each rider, even if he is an opponent, not to have to break his stride unless absolutely necessary. The second rider will also glance both ways, and if all is clear, will wave on the next person behind him. If someone realizes that a car is coming, he will yell *'Alt!'* so that the riders behind him know to come to a stop."

"At one point I noticed that some of the riders were reaching into the pockets that are stitched on the back of their biking jerseys, pulling out a granola bar of some kind. One of them turned to me and asked, 'You got something?'" I told him I'd eaten a sugar cube just before leaving. "Ach, that's not enough," he said. "Here, take half of this." And as he continued to pedal, he broke the snack bar in half and handed one part to me."

"One day while we were riding,' he said, "we went through a small town. Going through the winding streets I got separated from the rest of the group. Pretty soon, two of the cyclists came back to look for me. Then, they insisted on riding slightly ahead of me, so as to cut the wind resistance and give me a little break.

I thanked them, and they told me that this is standard practice. 'You don't think that one of us could win a race without the team, do you?' one of them smiled. 'Even the best of us could not keep up a winning pace for an entire race, unless from time to time we others rode ahead of him to give him a little breather.'"

"…the fruit of the Spirit is love, joy, peace, patience, kindness, generosity, faithfulness, gentleness, and self-control"

Galatians 5:22-23

The last fruit on Paul's list is 'self-control'; in Italian, *dominio di se*, ('dominion over oneself'). While the value of the first eight fruits seems obvious, especially for people living in Christian community, the purpose of the ninth fruit is less clear. At first glance, self-control appears to have less to do with others and more to do with… well, self.

More than half-way into worship, this small intercultural congregation had reached the time of intercessory prayers. When it comes to balancing our cultural traditions in worship, we can translate sermons, we can sing hymns in different languages, but praying together is more difficult than it sounds. The way we pray is, after all, very personal. Our preferences are rooted deep into our culture and character. To those who need an order of worship, for example, spontaneous praying can feel like chaos. To those who involve their whole bodies in their praying, a written liturgy can feel like a straight-jacket. To those who are accustomed to short prayers, the discomfort-stopwatch begins to tick after two or three minutes. And to those whose sense of liturgical time is less linear, concluding a prayer after two minutes may feel like stopping a movie at its opening credits. How can each one pray with integrity, while at the same time, respect the one with whom he/she shares a pew? It's not easy.

It was announced that there would be a time of 'spontaneous prayer' followed by a written one in Italian. The invitation unleashed a torrent of prayers and songs, some in Ghanaian Twi, one in Mauritius French, another in East African English. After several minutes everything became suddenly silent. I opened one eye to survey the congregation and saw that one of the African men was repeatedly slicing his hand through the air at waist level. The message to his fellow Africans was clear: that's enough… no more prayers… don't overwhelm our Italian brothers and sisters… we need to respect their tradition… they've got some prayers ready to read… give them space… this is their home, too.

A choir director once said that the split-second of silence after a piece is sung, when the echo of the last note still hangs in the air, is the choir's gift to God. That day, the space between those two prayers honoured both God and the other.

"Saul… Get up and go to the city, and you will be told what you are to do."

Acts 9:6

*"Ananias… Get up and to the street called Straight…
Look for a man named Saul"*

Acts 9:11

With the same number of verses to each, for some reason Saul's conversion story gets better press. Perhaps it's on account of its dramatic elements: blinding light, Saul's tumble to the ground, the deep base voice from the heavens. But who is Saul without an Ananias? A staggering blind man with scales over his eyes.

Ananias' story almost gets upstaged. Perhaps it is because he was already a disciple. After all, how much more changing would God expect him to do? He was already converted. But who is Ananias without Saul? An untroubled believer, never unsettled by anyone unlike himself.

This was the text for our Bible study class that morning. One of the women in the class commented: "I think the two men needed each other. One man had lived there a long time, and the other was from far away… a *straniero* (foreigner). But it was like God needed both of them to come together, or else it wouldn't have worked."

"A little like us," someone added, motioning toward the awaiting sanctuary. "If we always keep our same opinions of the Italians and don't realize they are changing, maybe we won't change either. And we can't keep saying to ourselves 'Oh, we're just poor, helpless *stranieri*', can we? Saul had to have the courage to step inside Ananias' house, and Ananias had to have the courage to let him in."

I had not heard conversion linked so tightly with community – not conversion in the individualistic way we often think about it, but a conversion that is mutual… perhaps not perfectly simultaneous, but with some kind of bold synchronicity. Two people, both taking new steps, however tentative, in a direction that leads to a street called Straight.

*"...the church which Christ has opened
to people of all ages, nations, and races..."*

From the United Methodist Baptismal Liturgy (5)

Everything was exotic: the smells, the sounds, the language, the climate. Partly because of the culture shock, partly because of jet lag, and partly because of the immediate impact of having landed in a foreign city half-way around the world, the Italian couple had not slept very well on their first night in Manila. But today was Sunday. They would catch up on sleep, maybe take a walk and acclimatize a bit before the big day tomorrow. They were apprehensive about all that would happen over the course of the next week.

While they had arrived as a couple, they would depart with one other person: a little boy they had seen only in photos. Soon they and their newly adopted son would be starting a life together back in Italy. But so many questions remained: How would they communicate? Would he want to go? How would he adjust to them? To Italy? How would they help him remember a culture they were only getting to know themselves?

It was just over a year ago when they had stood up in church and announced the adoption. After years in the process, the woman in the international adoption agency had asked them, "What about a Filipino child?" They had looked at one another in disbelief. Their Methodist congregation in Milano has many people from the Philippines. They could not help but think that God might be sending them a sign: that they could bring their adopted son home to a church which included people from his native country. Ever since their announcement, Filipino church friends had coached them, translated documents for them, shared books, taught them recipes and greetings, and pointed out landmarks on maps.

But now it was just the two of them – groggy, disoriented, nervous, and alone – in a foreign land on a Sunday morning.

Then came a knock at the door. It was the caretaker of the guest house: "There's someone here to see you," she said. "See us? Here? We don't know anyone here. It must be a mistake."

"OK," replied the caretaker, "I'll go straighten it out." A few minutes later, however, she returned. "No, they want to see Stefano and Patrizia. That is you, isn't it?"

They nodded and walked to the front gate. A small group of Filipino adults stood there smiling. "Hello," said one of the women. "I'm Sofia's sister. Sofia... from your church in Milano. She told us you were coming, and we thought you might want to come to church with us this morning."

"Parthians, Medes, Elamites, and residents of Mesopotamia, Judea and Cappadocia, Pontus and Asia, Phrygia and Pamphylia, Egypt and the parts of Libya belonging to Cyrene, and visitors from Rome, both Jews and proselytes, Cretans and Arabs – in our own languages we hear them speaking about God's deeds of power..."

Acts 2:9-11

The story of Pentecost would be a lot shorter if we took out that long list of places. The account rolls along – the Jewish people were all gathered in that locked room, they heard the sound of the rushing wind, they saw tongues of fire on their heads, they began speaking in languages not their own – and then the author seems to need to tell us everyone's place of origin. Wind, fire, voices – then a long digression to list all those hard-to-pronounce names. Almost as if an intriguing story is interrupted with a dull geography lesson.

Then we learn that all those places in that list represented the farthest reaches of the known world at that time (the Bible says, '*every* nation under heaven'). When God created the Church, the whole world was already present! The Church was, at its very beginning, multicultural. It was made up of people who would not have looked alike, were of different cultures, languages, histories, and backgrounds. They had all taken different paths to get to Jerusalem. Most likely, they came from places that the others in their community had never seen or visited. They may not have had much contact with one another prior to the day of Pentecost (which can always lead to careless stereotypes: '*You know those Elamites, they're all a bit dodgy...*').

On this particular Pentecost Sunday at the Methodist Church of Milan, where it is a long-held tradition for new members to join the church on Pentecost, the list in Acts 2:9-10 seemed to parallel those who took vows to uphold the church with their 'prayers, presence, gifts and service'.

Names like Saniata, Kojo, Adjetjy, Prempeh, Michele, Korang, Susan, Jesusa, Luca, Pangilinan, Paz, Maharajah, Jacob, Bonifacio and others. From places like Damortis, Saronno, Tarlac, Baguoio, Tamil Nadu, Kumasi, and others. Did the early church also have trouble pronouncing one another's names? Did members there, too, have to ask one another politely, "Excuse me, I didn't understand... would you repeat what you just said?" We know from subsequent stories in Acts that the early Christians had to decide whose hometown traditions made it into the new community.

Today, the long list in the Acts story seemed less like an add-on and more like a roll call. Not just *part* of the story, the list IS the story. What other list of that era would have grouped such an unlikely collection of places? Only the Holy Spirit could make Parthians, Medes, Africans, visitors and proselytes… one community.

Endnotes

Chapter 1, Hardly Together

1. Dietrich Bonhoeffer, *Life Together* (New York: Harper & Row Publishers, 1954), 48-49.

2. Bruce Springsteen, "Worlds Apart" (2002), *The Rising*, Columbia Records.

3. Baptismal Covenant I, *The United Methodist Book of Worship* (Nashville, Tennessee: The United Methodist Publishing House 1992), 37.

4. Elisabeth Rosenthal, "In Northern Italy, the Agony of Aging Not So Gracefully," *New York Times* (September 22, 2006).

5. George Weigel, *The Cube and the Cathedral – Europe, America, and Politics Without God* (New York: Basic Books, 2005), 166-167.

6. Joyce M. Bowers, ed., *Raising Resilient MK's, Resources for Caregivers, Parents, and Teachers* (El Cajon, California: E.D. Publishers, 1998), 55.

7. From John Wesley's Select Hymns, 1761, (*The United Methodist Hymnal*

8. (Nashville, Tennessee: The United Methodist Publishing House, 1989), vii.)

Chapter 2, Together, in our Fears

1. Martin Luther King, Jr., speech at King Chapel, Cornell College, Vernon, Iowa, October 15, 1962.

Chapter 3, Coming Together as Guests and Hosts

1. John Wesley, *Explanatory Notes on the Whole Bible* (Baker, 1996).

2. F. Belton Joiner, Jr., Gloria E. Bengston, Laurie J. Hanson, James Satter, Rebecca Lowe, eds., *The Unofficial United Methodist Handbook for Pastors* (Nashville, Tennessee: Abingdon Press, 2007), 119.

3. Photo from *La Repubblica* (December 11, 2007).

4. Jodi Kantor, quoting former White House chef Walter Scheib,"Where the Votes Are, So are All Those Calories," *New York Times* (November 23, 2007).

Chapter 5, Together, in the City

1. Henri Nouwen, *Clowning in Rome; Reflections on Solitude, Celibacy, Prayer, and Contemplation* (Garden City, New York: Images Books, 1979), 37.

2. Elisabeth Povoledo, "A Cinematic View of Italy as Morally Bankrupt," New York Times (November 23, 2006).

3. "O Come, O Come, Emmanuel," (9th century hymn), *The United Methodist Hymnal* (Nashville, Tennessee: The United Methodist Publishing House, 1989) 211, verse 6.

4. Phillips Brooks, "O Little Town of Bethlehem," (ca. 1868), *The United Methodist Hymnal* (Nashville, Tennessee: The United Methodist Publishing House, 1989) 230, verse 1.

Chapter 6, Together, in the Empire

1. Peter Berlin, "Root for your team, but nicely," *International Herald Tribune* (June 30, 2006).

2. Stanley Hauerwas and William H. Willimon, *Resident Aliens; Life in the Christian Colony* (Nashville, Tennessee: Abingdon Press, 1989), 12.

3. Luigi Barzini, *The Europeans* (New York: Simon & Schuster, 1983), 178-179.

4. Maisie Wilhelm, "If the jeans fit: Italy's youth play safe," *International Herald Tribune* (February 26, 2007).

Chapter 7, Together, When our Religious Labels Differ

1. Rumi, source unknown.

Chapter 8, Together, in Conflict

1. Jean Vanier, appeared in a 2002 issue of National Catholic *Reporter*.

2. Katie G. Cannon, *God's Fierce Whimsy* (New York: Pilgrim Press, 1985.

3. Susan McEwan (former community organizer with Dundonald Methodist Church and the Community Partners Project, Belfast,

Northern Ireland), "Across the Lines," *Corrymeela Connections*, Volume 8, Number 1, October 2004.

4. Margaret Thatcher Foundation web site (http://www.margaretthatcher.org), transcript of the BBC John Cole interview, December 17, 1984.

Chapter 9, Together, by Acts of Grace

1. Eric H.F. Law, *The Wolf Shall Dwell with the Lamb; A Spirituality for Leadership in a Multicultural Community* (St. Louis, Missouri: Chalice Press, 1993), 3.

2. Alan Richardson and John Bowden, eds., *The Westminster Dictionary of Christian Theology* (Philadelphia: The Westminster Press, 1983), 244-245.

Chapter 10, Together, Step by Step

1. Emily Townes, "A Conversation with Tex Sample and Emily Townes," *Alive Now; Growing Together in Faith*: *Differences*" (Nashville, Tennessee: The Upper Room, September/October 1995), 20.

2. Martin Luther King, Jr., address to the First Montgomery Improvement Association (MIA), Holt Street Baptist Church, Montgomery, Alabama, December 5, 1955.

3. Paul Tillich, *The Shaking of the Foundations*, semon entitled, "You are Accepted," (New York: Charles Scribner's Sons, 1948).

4. Stanley Hauerwas, class on Introduction to Christian Ethics, Duke Divinity School, Durham, North Carolina, 1988 (quote dependent on the memory of the author).

Chapter 11, Together, through *Carità*

1. Giorgio Tourn, with the collabouration of Giorgio Bouchard, Roger Geymonat, Giorgio Spini; Frank G. Gibson, Jr., ed., *You Are My Witnesses, The Waldensians across 800 years* (Torino: Claudiana, 1989), 203-206.

Chapter 12, Together, in the Spirit

1. Henri Nouwen, *The Life of the Beloved; Spiritual Living in a Secular World* (Chesnut Ridge, New York: Crossroad Publishing, 1992).

2. H. Ernest Nichol, "We've a Story to Tell to the Nations," (1896), *The United Methodist Hymnal* (Nashville, Tennessee: The United Methodist Publishing House, 1989) 569, chorus.

3. John Allen, *Rabble-Rouser for Peace, The Authorized Biography of Desmond Tutu* (New York: Free Press, 2006), 136.

4. Wiegel, 166-167.

5. Bengt Sundkler and Christopher Steed, *A History of the Church in Africa* (Cambridge: Cambridge University Press, 2000), quoted in John Allen, *Rabble-Rouser for Peace, The Authorized Biography of Desmond Tutu* (New York: Free Press, 2006), 29.

6. John Parker, "Advent a Time of Spiritual House Cleaning," *The Post and Courier* (Charleston, South Carolina, December 2, 2007).

7. James A. Simpson, *A Funny Way of Being Serious* (London: Steve Savage Publishers, 2005).

8. Roger J. Vanden Busch, "The Value of Silence in Quaker Spirituality," *Spirituality Today* (Winter 1985, Volume 37), 326-335.

Chapter 14, Together, following Jesus

1. Alexander Stille, *The Sack of Rome: How a Beautiful European Country with a Fabled History and a Storied Culture Was Taken Over By a Man Named Silvio Berlusconi* (New York: The Penguin Press, 2006), 74-79.

2. Isaac Watts, "Joy to the World," (1719), *The United Methodist Hymnal* (Nashville, Tennessee: The United Methodist Publishing House, 1989), 246, verse 1.

Chapter 15, Together, in the Body of Christ

1. Kahlil Gibran, *The Prophet*, (London: Wordsworth Classics of World Literature, 1923), chapter on marriage.

2. Parker Palmer, *The Promise of Paradox; A Celebration of Contradictions in the Christian Life* (San Francisco: Jossey-Bass, 1980).

3. Jean Vanier, source unknown.

4. Thomas Aquinas, source unknown.

5. Baptismal Covenant I, *The United Methodist Book of Worship*

Scripture quotations, unless otherwise noted, are taken from the *New Revised Standard Version Bible*, 1989, Division of Christian Education of the National Council of the Churches of Christ in the United States of America.

Other versions of scripture used:

Eugene H. Peterson The Message/Remix; The Bible in Contemporary Language, 2003, Colorado Springs, Colorado: Navpress.

Good News Bible, Good News Translation, 1992, New York: American Bible Society.

Holy Bible: New International Version, 1989, Grand Rapids, Michigan: Zondervan Publishers.

New Living Translation, 2007, Carol Stream, Illinois: Tyndale House Publishers, Inc.

The New American Bible, 1970, Catholic Biblical Association of America, Bishops' Committee of the Confraternity of Christian Doctrine, Paterson, New Jersey: St. Anthony Guild Press.

The New Testament of Our Lord and Saviour Jesus Christ, and Psalms, King James Version, 1971, New York, Thomas Nelson, Inc.

The Photographs

The photographs in this book were taken by the author, except for the following:

Pg 147: Orchestra conductor with baton; Gerard Fritz

Pg 171: Detail of Byzantine mosaic at San Vitale Basilica, Ravenna; http://gohistoric.com/

Pg 190: The Last Supper by Leonardo da Vinci; http://www.ilpadenghino.it/

Pg 197: Title page 'Together as the Body of Christ'; Roberto Tettamanzi

Pg 208: Milan Trams; Joop van Meer

The Author

A native of New Jersey, USA, David Markay is a graduate of Dickinson College and Duke University Divinity School. He was ordained in 1991 and has served in ministry in England, the United States, Lithuania and Italy. He currently serves in the Sheffield Circuit of the Methodist Church in Britain.

Other work by this author:

Lithographs from Lithuania; Crossings and Crosses
(2004, AuthorHouse)

CR

A tithe of the proceeds from the sale of this book will be donated to the *Opera per le Chiese Metodiste in Italia* (Methodist Church in Italy) in its continued work among immigrants.